One Man
and the
Mighty Mississippi

A SIXTY-YEAR ADVENTURE
ON THE
MISSISSIPPI AND OHIO RIVERS

by
Captain Norman Hillman

To my wife Ranell
for her patience and help
through the years

Contents

List of Photographs and Illustrations

Preface

My daughter, Stephanie, was a junior or senior in high school. I had just returned home after working a thirty-day cycle on the towboats. At the supper table, I was telling my wife and daughter of an incident that happened on the boat. My daughter excused herself, got up, and said, "Oh, Pop, I don't want to hear any of your old stories."

Two or three years later she was home from Purdue University for a weekend, and at the supper table she said, "Pop, tell us a story." I said, "I thought you were the one who didn't care for my stories." She had to write a theme by Monday when she returned to school, so she needed a story!

Years later, after I had retired from the Valley Line Company, Stephanie said, "Pop, you really should write down some of your experiences. You've seen the river change so much. The boats have changed from mostly steamboats to diesel-powered boats. When you're gone no one will remember."

At her urging I purchased a spiral notebook, and as I was piloting the *Queen* boats, each time I'd pass a location and recall an incident that happened near there, I jotted it down. This book is a collection of those stories covering sixty-plus years on the great Mississippi River system. Fifty-nine of those years I was licensed by the United States Coast Guard as a First Class Pilot and Master of Vessels of All Gross Tons on the Western Rivers, which include the Ohio, Mississippi, Illinois and any other river flowing to the Gulf of Mexico. I held a valid United States Coast Guard license from October 1939 to July 2000.

My original goal was to have a story so my grandchildren would know what their grandfather did for a living, but a number of people have urged me to write a book of my experiences. I hope the reader will enjoy my work.

Captain Hillman on watch.

Acknowledgments

I cannot thank my wife, Ranell, enough for the many hours and evenings she has spent by herself these past three years or so, while I was working on the computer and putting this manuscript together—and for putting me back to work on the manuscript whenever I became discouraged after goofing up.

I want to thank Jill Bolinger and Bob Capps for their assistance in getting me straightened out on the computer whenever I became stuck; Helene Schultz and her writing class for their help; and Ann Wolford and Herman Reitz for proofreading my material.

I want to thank my daughter, Stephanie, for encouraging me to put my experiences down on paper and for her work with the graphics and editing on the manuscript.

Introduction

Many people of the present generation are not aware of the significance of the mighty Mississippi River, the beautiful Ohio River and their many tributaries, and the impact and role they had on the founding and development of our great country. The early voyageurs, fur trappers and traders used canoes and bateaus to traverse these rivers. The immigrants soon followed, floating down the Ohio and Mississippi Rivers with all of their worldly goods tightly laced to their flatboats, hunting for new homes. About 1807, Robert Fulton built the first steamboat in America, named the *Clermont*. In 1811, the *New Orleans*, a paddlewheel boat, was built at Pittsburgh, and it showed that there could be two-way traffic on the rivers, since the steamboat could go upstream as well as down. The packet boats built after the *Clermont* could carry passengers as well as freight. Some of the packet boats in their heyday were very luxurious and elegant.

At this same time, the railroads were expanding all over this country, and they were not limited to where the water flowed. So after the Civil War, the steamboat packet trade went into a decline. There was coal business, bringing coal out of the Pennsylvania coal fields to the south. The coal barges were assembled and tows made up in the Pittsburgh area. The boats waited until there was a rise in the river level

Comparison of various modes of transportation

CARGO CAPACITY

BARGE
1500 TON
52,500 BUSHELS
453,600 GALLONS

15 BARGE TOW
22,500 TON
787,500 BUSHELS
6,804,000 GALLONS

EQUIVALENT UNITS

1 BARGE

15 JUMBO HOPPERS

1 TOW

2¼ UNIT TRAINS

EQUIVALENT LENGTHS

¼ MILE

15 BARGE TOW

2¼ MILES

2¼ UNIT TRAINS

JUMBO HOPPER CAR
100 TON
3,500 BUSHELS
30,240 GALLONS

100 CAR UNIT TRAIN
10,000 TON
350,000 BUSHELS
3,024,000 GALLONS

LARGE SEMI
26 TON
910 BUSHELS
7,865 GALLONS

58 TRUCKS

870 TRUCKS

34½ MILES
ASSUMING 150 FT.
BETWEEN TRUCKS

Iowa Department of Transportation

Prepared by:
Planning and Research Division

so they would have enough water to navigate in. Then they'd take off, hoping to go all the way to New Orleans on the rise. Before the construction of the locks and dams, without a rise, the river might not have enough depth to float the steamboats and their barges the entire distance to New Orleans.

In 1875, Congress authorized the Corps of Engineers to construct a series of locks and dams on the Ohio River to give boats enough water for year-round navigation. The construction of the first lock and dam was started on August 19, 1878, at Davis Island in the Pittsburgh area, and it went into operation on October 7, 1885. President Herbert Hoover presided over the dedication ceremony held upon completion of the Ohio River locks and dams in 1929. This system created a nine-foot channel from Pittsburgh to Cairo, Illinois.

By 1917 the Corps of Engineers had completed channels on the Mississippi River: the six-foot channel from St.Paul to St.Louis and the nine-foot channel from St.Louis to New Orleans. When America entered World War I, it was apparent that there was a serious need for bulk transportation. Mr. Edward F. Goltra wangled a contract from the government, and the government authorized the building of four steamboats and nineteen barges. Because all of the shipyards were working at capacity, the boats were built up the St. Croix River at Stillwater, Minnesota. They were not completed until after the end of the war, and because of a shallow channel and low water they were not successful operating on the Upper Mississippi River. They were moved to the Lower Mississippi River and worked in competition with the Federal Barge Line. After a lot of legal wrangling, Goltra's contract was broken and the boats and barges ended up in the Federal Barge Line fleet.

The Inland Waterways Corporation was formed in 1924 to take over the management of the Federal Barge Line, which developed a less-than-carload-lot business and had terminals scattered along both the Lower and Upper Mississippi River. Due to the increasing prosperity of the business, several privately owned companies got into the less-than-carload business: the Mississippi Valley Barge Line, the Kelly Barge Line (later called the American Barge Line), the Campbell Barge Line, and numerous others.

The Upper Mississippi River north of St.Louis was limited to about a three-foot draft of water; in the summertime, there was less water than that. Around 1907 Congress authorized a four-and-one-half foot-deep channel project on the Upper Mississippi, and before the project was very far along it was upped to a six-foot channel. Congress passed the Rivers and Harbors Act of 1930, which authorized the construction of a series of locks and dams to provide a nine-foot-deep channel on the Upper Mississippi River from St. Paul to St. Louis. The Corps of Engineers oversaw the construction of twenty-six locks and dams. The last two were Lock No. 22 at Clarksville, Missouri, and Lock No. 25 at Winfield, Missouri, which were completed in 1940.

The average layperson has no idea the benefit the nine-foot channel development was to this country during World War II. Numerous naval vessels and some deep sea vessels were built far inland, some as far inland as Savage, Minnesota. They were launched on the Minnesota River and were either towed or piloted to New Orleans, which is a deep water port. At Seneca, Illinois, on the Illinois River, a corn field was converted into a shipyard almost overnight, where 197 Landing Ship Tanks (LSTs) were built during World War II. Numerous submarines were built in Manitowoc, Wisconsin, and transported via a dry dock to the Gulf via Lake Michigan, the Illinois Waterway and the Mississippi River. The ex-Goltra steamboat *Minnesota* pushed the submarine dry dock during most of the war.

Since World War II, Mississippi River system traffic has greatly increased. Barges move millions of tons of bulk cargo each year. The Upper Mississippi River and the Illinois waterway are the leading source of export-bound grain in the United States. In 1996 approximately fifty-four percent of all United States corn exports and forty percent of all soybean exports were loaded in barges on these waterways above St. Louis, Missouri. These two rivers also serve as a major transportation corridor for other commodities, including fertilizer, coal, steel, cement and petroleum products.

Also, parts of space rockets are built in Huntsville, Alabama, and transported by barge to Cape Canaveral, Florida. The parts are too large to go by any other route. This would not be possible without the great Mississippi River system.

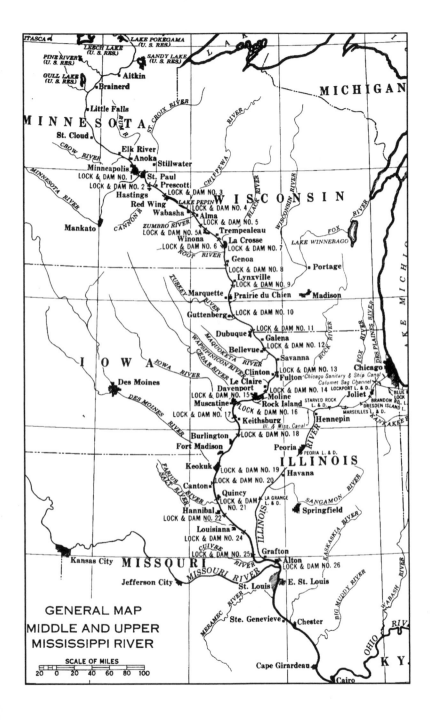

GENERAL MAP
MIDDLE AND UPPER
MISSISSIPPI RIVER

SCALE OF MILES
20 0 20 40 60 80 100

Western Rivers System

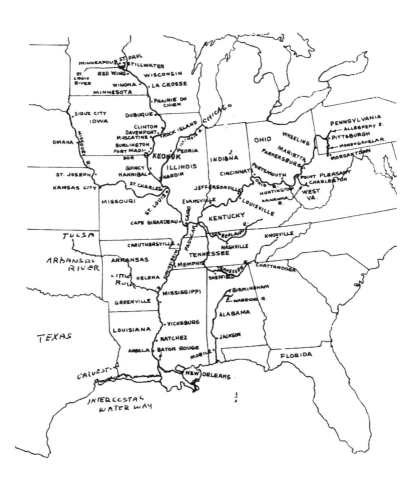

1 The Beginning of a Great Adventure

I graduated from Ottawa High School in June, 1936, in the middle of the Great Depression. During the Depression jobs were very hard to find. There were the Works Progress Administration and the Civilian Conservation Corps camps for young men, and a lot of men sold apples on a street corner trying to make enough to keep their families fed.

I was offered a job as a deckhand on a small boat called the *Robert R.* The *Robert R* originally belonged to the Chicago Sanitary District and was used as an inspection boat for the canal and the electrical power lines that ran alongside the canal from the powerhouse at Lockport, Illinois, to Chicago to power Chicago's streetlights. But her main claim to fame was her use by the Chicago politicians as a party boat.

The *Robert R* was seventy-two feet long and eighteen feet wide. Captain Bob Robertson bought her from the Sanitary District and repowered her with a 180-horsepower Superior Diesel engine. He ran her as a excursion boat for a couple of years, then decided there was more money in the towing business so converted her into a towboat at Ottawa, Illinois, during the spring of 1936. On the bow he constructed vertical bumpers called *towing knees* that allow a boat to push against a barge without running under it. He also built nice rooms inside for the crew. The boat already had a very efficient galley and dining room. I had been hanging around the *Robert R* after school and probably making a general nuisance of myself. For two summers I had worked as a dockboy for a ChrisCraft speedboat thrill ride at Starved Rock State Park and enjoyed every minute of it.

If I took the job on the *Robert R* I would have to miss my graduation exercises, because the boat was leaving on June 1 and graduation day was June 4. I didn't know what to do, so I asked my folks for their opinion. They said, "Ask Mr. H. D. Anderson." He was principal of my high school. Mr. Anderson said he hated to see me miss my graduation exercises, but the program was only a couple of hours long and I would get my diploma. The way the employment situation was, jobs were very scarce and if it were up to him, he would take the job—and that is what I did.

I started on the *Robert R* as a deckhand. The pay was one dollar a day for a twelve-hour day and no time off. If you wanted off, you quit and there were fourteen guys standing on the bank waiting to take your place.

The *Robert R* went to Lockport, Illinois, in June of 1936 and started towing sand and gravel from the Material Service Corporation plant at Lockport to their yards in Chicago. The first year we towed three wooden barges and had to pump them constantly, for they leaked like sieves.

Also, the sand and gravel was washed before it was loaded into the barges and the water drained into the bilge or bottom of the barge, so we had a lot of water to pump. Two of the barges had built-in pumps with old Chevrolet engines. My

M/V Robert R *as an excursion boat.* PHOTO BY AUTHOR

partner and I quickly learned the proper way to crank an old kicking engine. Once I thought my arm had been broken when one of the old beasts kicked me.

Eventually we started towing some steel barges, which cut our pumping time considerably. My partner and I were in seventh heaven, for we no longer had to fool with the pumps with the Chevy engines. We just used a small portable gasoline pump tp pump the bilges.

In August of 1937, our pilot quit. Since pilots were in very short supply and Captain Robertson owned the boat, he told me to give piloting a try. At this time, pilots on a diesel boat did not have to be licensed. I had been doing a lot of steering for Captain Robertson and was very lucky to have this kind of a break so young. The reason the pilot had quit was directly related to our running between the sand and gravel plant at Lockport and Material Service Yard No. 12 in Chicago, which was located on the south branch of the Chicago River in the middle of the stockyard district where the slaughterhouses were located. The meatpacking houses at this time

M/V Robert R *after being converted to a towboat.*

were dumping all of their effluent (waste) into the Chicago River, and Chicago was dumping all of its raw sewage into Lake Michigan or the Sanitary Canal, which flowed into the Des Plaines River and then the Illinois River. In the 1930s there were no sewage treatment plants in Chicago. It was an out-of-sight, out-of-mind mentality. We called the south branch of the Chicago River "Bubbly Creek," and the odor was almost unbearable.

It *was* unbearable for our pilot. We were in Bubbly Creek every day, arriving about nine in the morning and not leaving until about six in the evening, or whenever our barges were unloaded. Because of the stench, our poor pilot was not keeping any food down. He'd throw up his breakfast and couldn't eat any lunch or dinner. All he had was a little light lunch at midnight when he came on watch. He had to get off to survive.

One day we were lying at the Material Service dock in Bubbly Creek and a group of kids were teasing a wino with a wine

CHAPTER 1

M/V Robert R *pushing two gravel barges.*

bottle. They threw the bottle out into the middle of the creek and it stayed on top of the effluent and grease, which was about six inches thick. I couldn't believe my eyes when the wino swam out in that mixture to retrieve the wine bottle. I saw this scene repeated a couple of times while we were running up in this area. When the *Wm. T. Warner* started towing for the Material Service Corporation, they had a pilot from Memphis, Tennessee. On his first trip up Bubbly Creek he said, "If I ever fell in this, it would be the end of me." Sure enough, a few trips later he got off at yard No. 12 to go to the telephone; the boat was tied off to some empty barges, and while he was gone the wind blew the barges away from the dock. He came back and couldn't get on the barges or boat. The crew were all inside drinking coffee and they couldn't hear him hollering. He picked up a twelve-foot two-by-six plank, placed it against the empty barge, and started to crawl up it on his hands and knees. He was about halfway to the barge when the plank flipped and he went into Bubbly Creek. When he finally got onto the boat, he packed his clothes, caught a taxi to the railroad station, and took the first train back to Memphis. That was all of Bubbly Creek he wanted.

• • •

In late 1937, we started towing sand and gravel from the Chicago Sand and Gravel Company at Rockdale below Joliet, Illinois. Warner and Tamble, a towing company from Memphis, Tennessee, had come on the scene with the Wm. T. Warner and taken over most of the sand and gravel towing for the Material Service Corporation. The John I. Hay Company also got into the act and towing prices kept dropping until no one could make any money. In June of 1936, when we started towing for the Material Service Corporation, the rate was thirty to thirty-five cents a ton, depending on which yard we delivered to. By late 1937, the rate had dropped to a flat rate of ten cents a ton no matter which yard it was destined for.

Captain Robertson got out of the sand and gravel business and we started towing grain out of Havana and Pekin, Illinois, into South Chicago. We pushed two old wooden grain barges belonging to the Dewey Grain Company of Pekin. Being wooden barges, they had to be pumped out by hand. The pump was made from a four-inch rain downspout, with a pole down the middle and pieces of canvas and leather for a foot valve and lifting mechanism. You lifted the water out by working the pole up and down like an old creamery churn. It worked. After a few trips we replaced the wooden barges with two steel grain barges and cut down the time we spent pumping.

• • •

Just a short distance below the E. J. & E. railroad bridge there was a place everyone called "the Hump," and it was just that.

The channel above it was quite deep, and then it shoaled off very abruptly to a solid rock bottom. The river could not scour out because of the rock bottom. Consequently, the water came rushing down the river and jumped up over the rock to keep going, very much like a rapids. When the powerhouse at Lockport was running a lot of water you could actually see a hump in the water. Warner & Tamble installed a small flat (barge) with a gas winch and the end of the cable was tied off to a buried anchor on shore that we called a "dead man." They would drop the flat down about a thousand feet, tie on to a tow and pull the tow up over the hump. Once over the hump, the towboat could shove without assistance. Sometimes barges would be tied off at this location, and a couple of boats that I knew of would land alongside and exchange their old, worn-out lines for the good ones on some one else's barges. I can say we were never guilty of that thievery.

• • •

When I was working for Bob Robertson on the *Robert R*, we had a tow of a dredge and assorted equipment belonging to the Great Lakes Dredge and Dock Company from Peoria Lock to Chicago. The dredge had been dredging the cofferdam from around the construction site of the new Peoria Lock. The cofferdam had been built so the new lock could be built inside a dry hole.

We were assisted in pushing the dredge and its equipment up the river by the *Anna M*, a twin-screw, wooden hull boat, about 240 horsepower. The *Anna M* vibrated so badly that the *Robert R* also shook, and we were not even against the *Anna M*, just faced up to the same barge. I don't know how her crew stood it. We did deliver the dredge to Chicago

M/V Anna M
*cut down by
windowpane ice
rubbing against
her wooden hull.*
PHOTO BY AUTHOR

without a mishap, but we joked that the *Anna M's* engineer
had to stand between the engines with a hand braced on each
engine to keep the cylinder heads from hitting each another
and cracking their tops. Not quite the truth, but it was almost
that bad.

• • •

The *Robert R* was coming up the river abreast of Pekin, Illinois, one trip and the *Anna M* was aground with a couple
of loaded grain barges. We stopped to help, and in the
process of helping them off the ground, we pulled a cavel
(fitting) off one old barge. Would you believe their boss
tried to bill the *Robert R* for the damage! That was the last
time we ever stopped to help them. In those days it was
common practice to stop and give help to anyone in trouble. We didn't have to notify the office, for the next time
we might be the one needing the assistance. This was a
you-scratch-my-back-I'll-scratch-yours policy and it worked
very well.

In January of 1940, the *Anna M* was cut down by windowpane ice above Marseilles, Illinois, on the Illinois River. (Windowpane ice is just about as thick as a pane of glass and will

cut through a wooden hull in no time.) She sank at Kickapoo Bend, and although she was raised, she didn't run much after that.

One year a yacht owner waited until too late in the fall to take his very nice wooden hull yacht to Florida from Chicago. He was about halfway across Peoria Lake when the yacht was cut down by the windowpane ice and sank.

2 The M/V Superior Diesel Comes on the Scene

Shortly after I started piloting for Captain Robertson, he bought a small diesel boat and converted it to a towboat. We built a set of towing knees on her, installed two hand capstans on her foredeck, built some rooms for the crew and fixed up the galley and dining area. Also we installed a ram for a hydraulic pilothouse so the pilot could see over an empty barge; after piloting on the *Robert R*, where we had to stand out in the weather, the hydraulic pilothouse was pure pleasure. The boat was named *Superior Diesel*, and she had a single screw (propeller), powered by a seventy-horsepower Superior Diesel engine. A nice little boat.

Captain Robertson needed a captain for the *Superior Diesel*. A license was not required on a diesel boat at this time, so I was hired as captain and John Honeyman was hired as my pilot. We carried two engineers, who helped out on deck at the locks and landings, two deckhands, and one cook. We made a few trips with the *Superior Diesel* towing two grain barges from the Dewey Grain elevator at Pekin to South Chicago. At times we were overloaded. We didn't throw any fish out on the bank, but managed to get the job

M/V Superior Diesel *dry-docked in Chicago.*

done without too much double-tripping. Then we started towing steel from the Carnegie-Illinois steel plant in South Chicago to Moline, Illinois, for the International Harvester Corporation. The *Robert R* was too big to run through the Hennepin Canal efficiently, but the *Superior Diesel* was just the right size for the job. We pushed one barge 130 feet long by 30 feet wide from South Chicago to the International Harvester Plant at Moline, Illinois. We ran in this trade for the season, or as long as the Hennepin canal was open, usually from April to November. We ran down the Illinois River to about Bureau, Illinois, then through the Illinois-Mississippi Canal, commonly known as the Hennepin Canal, to the Mississippi River. The canal entered the Mississippi just below the mouth of the Rock River. We then ran up the Mississippi to Moline, Illinois.

The Hennepin Canal was seventy-five miles long and had thirty-two locks. The gates and valves were operated by hand.

We had to double-lock every lock, and the lock size was 170 feet long by 35 feet wide. Double-locking means that we'd put our barge into the lock chamber, knock the boat loose, and back the boat out of the lock. The lockmen would close the gates and drop or raise the barge to the next level. We'd pull the barge out of the lock and tie it off to the lock wall. The lockmen would then raise or lower the water in the lock chamber in order to lock the boat through. We'd face up to the barge and push it to the next lock.

At first we had to pull the barges out of the locks by hand, which meant putting a rope over your shoulder and leaning into it until the barge started to move. When the wind was blowing it could be quite a struggle. Eventually, Captain Robertson found a one-cylinder gas engine at a junkyard and we used it to run a spool or drum. The assembly worked like a capstan and it was a big help. We'd move the rig from barge to barge with the aid of a couple of planks. The Hennepin Canal had thirty-two locks, and if your hands didn't fit a crank handle when you started in the canal, they sure did when you got to the other end. We got a break at some of the locks because the upper gates were solid and were raised and lowered by regulating the water coming into a built-in tank. The gates were designed by a Corps of Engineers man named Marshall. The boat crew had to help the lockmen crank the other gates and valves open and shut. About eight or ten of the locks were only about a half mile apart, so after locking all morning, we could look back at the canal and it looked like a flight of stairs—a flight of water stairs.

Fifty-eight bridges crossed the canal, a number of them lift-type bridges owned by farmers who had land on both sides of the canal. All of them were opened or shut or lifted by hand-

M/V Superior Diesel *locking at Lockport Lock.*

cranked winches. The Rural Electric Authority (REA) had not been around long enough to bring electricity into this part of the country. The lockmen had to open all the locks and bridges for us. They worked in pairs: two prepared the lock and helped us to lock through while the other two drove ahead and had the next bridge open or lock ready when we arrived.

• • •

In the summer of 1938, while running the Hennepin Canal on the Superior Diesel, we locked through Lock No. 32 about two a.m. and into the Mississippi River. Just after we left the lock a fog set in, shutting pilot John Honeyman out. He couldn't see anything but did manage to push in against a wing dam in the Mississippi River, abreast of the lock. A short time later the lockman, pulling a yawl, came alongside He could hear our engines running so knew where we were. He wanted to know if his cat was aboard the barge. We had a flat deck barge in tow, loaded with steel rods and flat bars. We called for the cat up and down the barge, but no luck.

When the fog cleared we went on to Moline, Illinois, getting in Friday evening. The dock crew unloaded part of the

Hulk of M/V Superior Diesel *after the fire.*

load Saturday, then knocked off for the weekend. Monday they finished, and when they were down to the last few bundles, here came the cat, scared to death and almost starved to death. We took her back to the galley and fed her milk and meat. When we got back down to Lock No. 32 late Monday evening, we put the cat off on the lock wall. She was one happy cat to see the familiar surroundings. Though before this we had always had to throw her off the barge before we left the lock, she never tried to get on the barge again—she'd had all the towboating she wanted.

An incident I well recall happened after I had made several trips through the Hennepin Canal with good luck. On this trip we had come down the Illinois River, which was rising, and there was a strong current. I tried to steer into the canal as I had done on the other trips, when there was not much current. I missed the mouth of the canal and ran aground on the bank below the canal. After unhooking the towboat ("knocking the boat out of tow"), we carried a line across the river and tied one end the line to a tree on the other bank. On the barge we had a hand-operated winch called a stump-puller. We tied the other end of our line into this winch. We had just got a good strain on the line when another towboat, either the M/V *Franklin D. Roosevelt* or M/V *Tom Sawyer,* came around the corner. We had to pull the line in so the towboat could go by and then hook the rope up again. Finally, with the help of our stump-puller, we managed to get our barge off the bank. I learned my lesson—I didn't try steering into a canal with a lot of headway again.

Only one other boat was running through the canal then—the M/V *Joan Dalton,* a 120-horsepower, single-screw boat owned by Captain Bill Michaelson. She didn't make any better time than we did, for you can only go so fast in such a restricted channel. I was one of the last pilots to work the Hennepin Canal. The Corps of Engineers closed it in about 1954 because there was not enough traffic to justify keeping it open. Later the canal property was turned over to the State of Illinois. The *Superior Diesel* caught fire and burned at Hennepin, Illinois, in November of 1938. I was severely burned in the fire and spent sixteen days in the Spring Valley, Illinois, hospital. At first the doctors gave me a fifty percent chance of recovering from my burns, but I recovered except for a few scars. Unfortunately, I lost pictures and negatives of every lock and bridge on the Hennepin Canal that were on the *Superior Diesel* when she burned.

3 The M/V Bonny R

After recuperating from the burns I received when the *Superior Diesel* burned at Hennepin, Illinois, I returned to work on the *Robert R* in late December, a little weak but ready to work. When we were not busy making a trip with the *Robert R* into Chicago, the entire crew worked on building a new boat. We were constructing it on the left descending bank below Rockdale, Illinois, just above Hunting Lodge Bend. The *Robert R*'s hull was in very poor condition and leaked like a sieve, requiring constant pumping. Captain Robertson knew he would have to replace the *Robert R*—he was just hoping

M/V Bonny R *under construction across from Hunting Lodge Bend.* PHOTO BY AUTHOR

M/V Bonny R.   PHOTO BY AUTHOR

she would last until we had the new boat ready to go.

In February, I went on the *M/V Edw. W. Bilhorn*, a 240-horsepower twin-screw boat, to replace the pilot, Red, who had been injured when he fell into an empty barge. I was on the *Bilhorn* for three weeks until Red returned. The boat had an up-and-down pilothouse of sorts so the pilot could see over high barges. It was cranked up and down by a deckhand using hand winches, and the engines were controlled with hand clutches. The clutches were so hard to lock into gear that you had to kick the levers very hard with your feet to make them lock into place. You really had to be a monkey to handle her.

M/V Edw. W. Bilhorn   PHOTO BY AUTHOR

4 *Steamboat Elsie*

In 1937 there was a woman who lived at Henry, Illinois, mile 196.0 on the Illinois River. She was known by all the river people as "Steamboat Elsie." She was a beautician and her husband, whom everybody called "Hubby," was a barber. They owned a small beauty and barber shop uptown.

Hubby's hobby was building a one-room cottage on a piece of property he and Elsie owned on the riverbank at the lower end of Henry. He bought old farm buildings, tore them down, and used the lumber to build the cottage. They stayed in it during the summertime for a couple of years and liked it so well they decided to live there year-round, so they moved into the cottage and rented their house out. The first year they lived in the cottage, the old highway swing bridge and Henry lock were still in operation. Boats had to whistle for an opening or for lock passage. Then the state replaced the bridge with a high bridge and the old Henry lock, which was just above the bridge, was taken out of service, so boats did not have to whistle for an opening for either the lock or the bridge.

Steamboat Elsie wrote to the *Waterways Journal*, a well-known river trade magazine, asking the boats passing by Henry

Steamboat Elsie Longman.
PHOTO BY AUTHOR

to please continue to whistle, as there were many people in Henry who enjoyed hearing them. Most of the boats at this time were steam-powered and had very pretty whistles. Some of the pilots complied with her request and some did not, so Steamboat Elsie started baking cakes—nice large cakes and tiny cupcakes. She boxed them up and Hubby lowered them from the bridge the next time the boat came through. The large cake was marked "To the pilot who whistled" and the cupcake was marked "To the pilot who did not whistle." Soon all the boats were whistling at Henry, Illinois. We also enjoyed the homemade caramel popcorn balls she dropped to us.

In 1937, The Ohio River Company started towing coal from Havana, Illinois, to Chicago for the Commonwealth Edison Company's power plants. The boats in those days did not have any radio communication except for the Federal Barge Line Company boats, which carried a radio operator and used Morse code. Since it took some time to push the seventy-five miles from Peoria lock to Starved Rock lock, the dispatchers who knew Steamboat Elsie started calling her and asking her to relay messages to boats they wanted to contact.

Steamboat Elsie used a very large megaphone to hail the boats and transmit the messages. I received messages from her a number of times.

Steamboat Elsie's cottage.

Elsie would not accept any pay for this service, so at Christmastime over the years, the dispatchers for the Ohio River Company, the Central Barge Company and the John I. Hay Company got together and gave the Longmans a bedroom set, a dining room set, a living room set and kitchen appliances. Hubby added more rooms to the cottage to hold all the furniture. After the house was more than furnished, the dispatchers gave them clothing, fur coats, suits, nice dresses, everything for a nice wardrobe.

Even after radios came into use in the early 1940s, the reception sometimes was not good, so everyone continued to use Steamboat Elsie's service. Hubby also constructed a large stone lighthouse next to the cottage that was on the Corps of Engineers navigation charts for many years.

It did not matter to Steamboat Elsie or Hubby if you were a captain, pilot, engineer, deckhand, cook or mess boy; if you went to Henry, Illinois, to catch a boat, you had to go to Elsie's to wait for the boat. She would not hear of anyone waiting at the hotel. She certainly was the friend of all river people. Steamboat Elsie died of cancer in May 1945.

CHAPTER 4

5 The Andersons of California

One day in the spring of 1938, I was southbound on the *Superior Diesel*. We had two empty grain barges in tow and were running between Pekin, Illinois and South Chicago in the grain trade for the Dewey Grain Company of Pekin, Illinois. As we passed Henry, Illinois, Steamboat Elsie hollered over that there was a couple by the name of Anderson from California in a flatboat just below the bend at Henry Island who might appreciate a tow across Peoria Lake. They were just floating with the current; they had no motive power, just two big sweeps (oars). Actually, the sweeps were two wide boards fastened to

Leona and Andrew Anderson of California.   PHOTO BY AUTHOR

21

the ends of long poles. They worked because there was not much current in the Illinois River at this time. The Andersons had built their flatboat in Chicago and were planning to sell it in New Orleans when they got there, just like a lot of the early settlers did when the country was first being opened up.

When we caught up to the Andersons, I asked them if they would like a tow to Peoria, an offer they gladly accepted. We towed them across Peoria Lake to Peoria and found out later that this was the only tow they accepted all the way to New Orleans.

They arrived safely in New Orleans and were able to sell their boat and return to California, having had a wonderful trip and an adventure with loads of memories. After I was married, my wife kept in contact with the Andersons by mail for a number of years.

6 The Sea Wolf

At the start of World War II, I took a job as a trip-pilot to take a yacht called the *Sea Wolf* from Joliet, Illinois, to St. Louis, Missouri. A trip-pilot contracts to work a certain number of days or to pilot a vessel from one point to another. He is not a full-time employee of the company or boat.

The *Sea Wolf* was 120 feet long, with two 600-horsepower Winton diesel engines driving twin screws (propellers), and she carried a crew of thirteen. The boat drew nine feet of water, and because the Illinois is a small, shallow river, we had to be very alert so she wouldn't take a run and dive for the shore. The master (captain in charge of the vessel), an old blue water sailor, wanted us to use a wheelsman (a deckhand who does the steering), but my partner and I soon found out we had to do our own steering. The wheelsman would not catch the dive for shore soon enough and we had a couple of close calls before we took over and did our own steering.

St. Louis gage read "zero" at this time. A gage is a reference point that has been established by the weather bureau to tell how much water is in the river at that point, and it shows whether the water level is rising or falling. The river

The Sea Wolf.

gage is read every morning by the weather bureau and the reading is broadcast by the United States Coast Guard to all boats at a scheduled time each day. There are gage boards located at various places along the river where the gage reading is also posted. The numerals on the gage board are large enough so that pilots can read them as they pass by.

River pilots use the gage readings to tell how much water covers a sand bar. Most pilots keep a "bar book" and record in it how much water it takes to cover certain sandbars, hurdles or rock wing dams. For example, if a sandbar was covered with water when the St. Louis gage read sixteen feet and the St. Louis gage now reads twenty-eight feet, the pilot knows there are twelve feet of water over the bar. If his vessel has a nine-foot draft, he can run over the bar safely. When the St. Louis gage read zero, there was just nine feet of water over the bedrock at the Chain-of-Rocks, a rock bottom extending all the way across the river just above St. Louis.

Captain Jim Lawrence was the other pilot on the *Sea Wolf.* Pilots on the river usually stand six hour watches: six a.m. to noon, noon to six p.m., six p.m. to midnight, midnight to six a.m. The master of the yacht would not let us run at night. He was an old deep sea captain, licensed for both steamships and sailing vessels, but was scared to death in close channels like we have on the river. Before the sun went down, we had to find a safe spot, out of the way of any barge traffic, and drop the anchor for the night. I think the master, besides being scared in close channels, also thought he would lose his crew if we tied up at a dock where the crew could go to town— and that could easily have happened.

Jim Lawrence did not know much about the Chain-of-Rocks channel, and none of the *Sea Wolf*'s crew knew how to use or read a lead line. (A lead line is a small rope about the size of a clothesline with fathoms marked by pieces of cloth or leather.) The man using the lead line can tell how deep the water is and call the figure out to the pilot. A piece of leather with two tails means twelve feet or "mark twain." Ten-and-a-half feet was called out as a "quarter less twain," thirteen-and-a-half feet as a "quarter twain," and fifteen feet as a "half twain." A piece of leather with three tails was placed at three fathoms (eighteen feet). At nine feet, fifteen feet and twenty-one feet, a piece of cloth was worked into the lead line so

⚓

SINGING OUT THE LEAD LINES

Today, I doubt if you could find anyone who knows how to read a lead line, even on a towboat. Everyone uses the fathometer, an electronic sounding device.

The oldtimers used to sing out the readings on a lead line and it was something to hear. I was fogbound below Turkey Island on the Illinois River and holding up by pushing into the bank. The steam towboat Gold Shield, *with an entirely black crew aboard, was coming up the river, towing blackstrap molasses from New Orleans to Peoria for the Commercial Solvents Corporation. Two deckmen were on the head of the tow, one on either side, leading. Could those men ever sing out the lead! I wish I had a tape recording of their voices, but even without one, I'll never forget that sound.*

that a leadsman could tell by feel, even at night, what depth he was finding and call it out to the pilot. Twenty-four feet or more was called out as "no bottom." The weight on the end of the lead line was made from a piece of pipe about six inches long, filled with lead except at the very bottom, which was open so that when the leadsman plumbed the river bottom it would pick up a small amount of material and he could tell if it was a mud, sand, or rock.

I had Jim do the leading for me and we got over the Chain-of-Rocks without knocking a hole in the bottom of the *Sea Wolf*. Several years later the construction of Locks No. 27 and the Chain-of-Rocks Canal by the United States Corps of Engineers did away with the necessity of running through the Chain-of-Rocks. A few years after the canal and locks were built, a fixed dam was installed so we could not run through the Chain-of-Rocks even if we wished to at high water. The fixed dam also backed up water to Lock No. 26, which did away with the problem of getting over the gate sills there.

We managed to get the *Sea Wolf* to St. Louis safely. She was en route to Miami, Florida, to be turned over to the United States Coast Guard to use as a submarine chaser. She belonged to the publisher of a Cleveland, Ohio, newspaper and she was luxurious. When I was aboard her she had teakwood decks, real china dishes and fancy silverware. I'm sure that all changed when the Coast Guard took over and everything was painted battleship gray.

Close Calls

During 1937 and early 1938, the *Robert R* towed grain from the Havana, Illinois, grain elevators to South Chicago. This was before the Peoria Dam was in operation—before the Peoria

Lock and Dam pool was filled. (The area above a dam where the water is held back forms a lake called a "pool.")

When we started towing grain barges we had difficulty seeing over the barges when they were empty, so we put a pilot wheel on top of the pilothouse of the *Robert R*, connecting it to the pilot wheel in the pilothouse with a chain arrangement. We also put some pull cords up there so we could ring the bells in the engine room to signal the engineer since the boat did not have a engine room telegraph. The arrangement worked fine except that it was out in the weather and in the wintertime it got mighty cold with no heat, not even a foot warmer. We also had to stay alert or get our heads knocked off by a low bridge. I never did get hit, but came too close for comfort a couple of times.

When we ran up the Sag Canal at night we rigged an incandescent searchlight on a stand for the man who was on top of the empty barge giving signals to the pilot in the pilothouse. One night I was on the barge and must have dozed off. We had been working very long shifts—eighteen hours at times. Bob, who was piloting, hollered at me just as I was about to get clobbered by a bridge. I ducked just in time.

• • •

Once I was trying to shove two barges of grain up through the Franklin St. bridge in Peoria with the *Superior Diesel* and stalled out with a fair current running. The *Franklin D. Roosevelt* of the Federal Barge Line came up behind me and the pilot, seeing my predicament, had his crew hang some "possums" (bumpers) over the head of his barge, eased up against me, and pushed me out of the bridge. It worked, and it saved us from having to drop back out of the bridge and double-trip the bridge. It also put us out of the *Roosevelt*'s way.

• • •

When I was pilot on the *Robert R*, I brought out all the steel from South Chicago for construction of the dam at Lock and Dam No. 25. We turned the barges over to the Str. *Transporter* at Joliet, Illinois, and Captain Birch McBride, master of the *Transporter*, took the steel on to the dam construction site on the Upper Mississippi River.

When I saw the first bargeload of steel for us to pick up at the Carnegie-Illinois steel plant, I knew there was no way it would go under the Indiana Avenue bridge, because the bridge had heavy braces that extended several feet below its floor. The dock foreman, whom I had to hunt up in the steel plant at one a.m., assured me that the barge would pass under the bridge. To convince me, he showed me the loading blueprint. The way the barge was loaded, it had to go directly under the bridge in such a manner that the braces would fit between the steel pieces with just a few feet of leeway. It *did* fit, but what a nervewracking job! We took several bargeloads out and were successful, with no damage to the bridge, cargo or my nerves.

7 The Central Barge Company

Mr. A. M. Thompson told me this story about forming the Central Barge Company. He owned the La Crosse Dredging Company and had done a lot of work on the nine-foot channel project on the Upper Mississippi River. He was sitting around with some of his cronies—Glen Traer, L. P. Runkel, A. H. Truax and A. C. Ingersoll, Sr.—and said, "We've built ourselves a river, now what are we going to do with it?" The result of the discussion was the formation of the Central Barge Company.

In 1938 they chartered an old boat, the Str. *Steel City,* and ran her while they were having the Str. *Alexander Mackenzie* and thirty barges built. They also bought the M/V *W. A. Shepard* from the American Barge Line Company and the M/V *Kosmos* from the Kosmosdale Cement Company.

Mr. Ingersoll owned the M/V *Kenton* and put it into the company as his share. I was lucky enough to start working for them when they first started out and they were great people to work for.

One day we were working on the new boat for Captain Bob Robertson, and Lynn Childs of the Central Barge Company called and asked Bob if I was real busy, because he needed a pilot for the *Kenton*. The pilot on the *Kenton* had had a bad accident when he tried to drive two loaded barges into Lock No. 26 with a lot of outdraft at the head of the lock chamber. He missed and hit the lock's outside bullnose, one barge breaking loose and going into the lock chamber, almost hitting the lower lock gates. The result was that he either quit or was fired.

I took the Santa Fe Railroad train from Joliet to Alton, Illinois, and then took a taxi to Lock No. 26. The lockmen told me the *Kenton* was probably at the Shell Oil dock in Wood River, Illinois, taking fuel. I had no idea where either Wood River or the Shell Dock was located. It was going to cost me ten cents to take the Illinois Traction Railroad electric car to Wood River, and I only had ten cents in my pocket. I decided to get a bowl of chili with my dime and wait in the park across from the lock. It was a warm April evening, so I lay down and catnapped on the grass off and on until the *Kenton* arrived about three a.m. and I was able to go aboard. I certainly would not try sleeping in the park today, for I would probably get hit in the head or worse!

The Kenton was fifty-five feet long, about eighteen feet wide, and was powered with a 150-horsepower Fairbanks-Morse engine. Some months earlier I had helped construct the upper cabin on the *Kenton,* so I knew she had cozy living quarters. The whole crew slept in one room on the second deck. The toilet and shower were in the engine room, and she did have a galley. The *Kenton* carried a crew of seven consisting of a captain, a pilot, two engineers, two deckhands and a cook.

On that first trip northbound with two empty grain barges, en route to Muscatine, Iowa, when we arrived at Lock No. 24, the dam was still under construction, so we had to try to

M/V Kenton, *Captain Ingersoll waving from the pilothouse*

shove through the open lock chamber. They were not using the lock gates yet and we were unable to shove through the swift current in the chamber. Half of the river was coffer-dammed off and all the water had to come through the open section and the lock chamber. It made for a very swift river. We teamed up with another boat that was having the same difficulty; the M/V *Jane Rhea* was a little sternwheel boat, probably about 200 horsepower. Together we got each other's barges through the lock chamber.

Above Lock No. 19, we were below Montrose, Iowa, and Nauvoo, Illinois, when the wind blew us into the Iowa shore. We ended up on a submerged concrete wall, which I later found to be part of the original canal around the Des Moines Rapids. No damage was done, but this was a good lesson, and I now knew what was under the water at that spot. We eventually arrived at Muscatine, Iowa, with our two empty barges. The barges were loaded with shelled corn at the McKee Grain elevator. They were destined to go up the Tennessee River for the broiler plants in Georgia. After the barges were loaded we departed southbound. (A broiler plant raises chickens for fast food restaurants.)

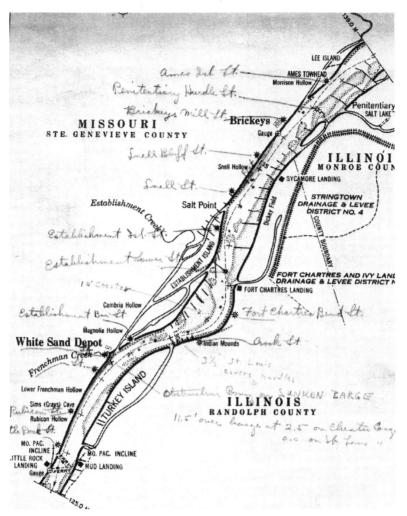

A typical river chart issued by the United States Corps of Engineers, 1940.

To say we were lost is an understatement, since I had never been below St. Louis and neither had my pilot. The charts we were using were not very good and very crude by today's standard. Captain Connie Ingersoll came aboard at Lock No. 26 to stand a pilot watch. I told Connie that we did not have a yawl (rowboat) on the *Kenton* and that we should have one, especially since we were going to Cairo and the river was high, around thirty feet on the St. Louis gage.

Thirty feet is flood stage on the St. Louis gage—when the water starts going over the top of the normal riverbank.

It was about midnight when we departed the lock. The Blaske Barge Line had two steamboats laid up at their landing just below Lock No. 26. Connie backed the *Kenton* in alongside the Str. *Elsie Marie.* There was no watchman aboard, so he simply had our deckhands take the yawl from the Str. *Elsie Marie.* He said, "Oh, I'll call Captain Blaske and tell him what we have done." We did return the yawl when we came back up the river. I heard later that Captain Blaske wasn't too happy about the deal.

Captain Ingersoll stood the night watches going down and I stood the daylight watches. Connie got messed up just above Cairo, Illinois, at Elzia Point and ran out into the willows above Angelo Towhead. When we stopped there were willow trees all around us We were able to get the *boat* out of the willows, but unable to get the *barges* out. The water was high and the barges were not actually aground, just stuck on top of the willow trees.

At that time there was only one small steam tug at Cairo, the *Susie Hazard.* She came up and helped, and together we were able to get the barges off. We had damaged our propeller trying to get the barges off the willows, so we had to go to the Mound City Marine Ways at Mound City, Illinois, to be pulled out of the water for wheel repairs.

The Mound City Marine Ways were not used very much, so the officials there really had to hunt to find two teams of

M/V Kenton *on the Mound City Marine Ways.*   PHOTO BY AUTHOR

horses to go around and around on the winches to pull us out of the water. It was an interesting procedure.

Marine ways are a set of rails, like railroad tracks, that run down a bank to a river. The vessel being pulled out sits on cradles that ride on the rails. Present-day marine ways use electric motors instead of horses. My understanding was that the Mound City Marine Ways had been in this same spot at the time of the Civil War and that numerous Union gunboats had been built at the shipyard during that war.

After going to Cairo on the *Kenton*, we came back up the Mississippi River and went up the Illinois River to Joliet, Illinois. Northbound, we were the first towboat to go through the new Kampsville Lock at Kampsville, Illinois, on the Illinois River. Southbound we had locked through the old lock chamber.

At Joliet, Captain Robertson wanted me back on the *Bonny R,* his new boat. On the *Bonny R* I made my first trip down the Illinois River and up to Quincy, Illinois, on the Mississippi

CHAPTER 7

River. In the Quincy vicinity the *Bonny R* threw two blades off the bronze propeller because of a manufacturing defect and we had to lay up until we could get a new wheel.

At this time, Lynn Childs of the Central Barge Company called and asked if I would work for them regularly. I talked it over with Bob Robertson and he said I'd better take the job because the Central Barge Company could pay me more than he could afford.

When I first went piloting for Bob, he was paying me $60.00 a month. At the Central Barge Company I was paid $150.00 a month, and a few months later my pay was raised to $300.00 a month, which seemed like a fortune. In the summer of 1939, I went from Joliet, Illinois, to Cairo, Illinois, again on the *Kenton*. Then I made a couple of trips from St. Louis to Cairo and a trip up the Ohio and Cumberland Rivers to Nashville, Tennessee.

We had two loads of shelled corn going to Nashville. All the lock machinery on the Cumberland River locks, both the gates and the valves to let the water in and out of the lock chambers, were operated by hand. We were sadly overloaded, as the *Kenton* was only 150 horsepower. We were not moving very fast—we surely didn't throw any fish out on the bank! This trip one of our barges was drawing eight and a half feet and we came to a bar with only eight feet of water over it. We had to tie the heavy barge to a tree and go to Nashville with the one barge we could get over the bar.

At Nashville we picked up a derrick boat and an empty barge to lighten the heavy load into. For insurance reasons we had left a man with the heavy barge. One deckhand refused to stay—the rest of the crew had been filling him full of tales about Kentucky moonshiners and had him scared of his own shadow. The cook had volunteered to stay with the barge if this man would cook on the boat in his place. The *Kenton* was no sooner out of sight when the farmer whose property the barge was tied to showed up. He said to our man, "You don't want to sit down here for a week. Come up to the house." He ended up eating all of his meals with the family, who took him to town on Saturday and even paid his way to the movie—to which the cook took the man's teenage daughter. The cook really lived high on the hog for the week we were gone. The poor guy who was cooking on the boat didn't fare so well—the crew complained the whole week. They said he couldn't even boil water to suit them.

After we got both barges to Nashville and they were unloaded, we had five empty barges to take downriver. I received a call from the superintendent of the Nashville Shipyard asking me to take another barge out with me. He was very eager to get the barge moved. I told him I was already overloaded. He asked me what kind of a boat I had and how much tow. I told him and he said, "Good luck," and hung up. We made it out of the Cumberland River safely with the help of the Good Lord.

• • •

A few weeks later, I shifted over to the *W. A. Shepard,* a 1350-horsepower, twin-screw boat running from Havana, Illinois, to Joliet, Illinois, on the Illinois River in the Commonwealth Edison Company coal trade. Captain L. J. Sullivan was master and Captain Don Gordon was the other pilot. Two months after I went on the *W. A. Shepard,* the company did away with the masters and only had a master-pilot and a pilot aboard. Because there were too many pilots, I was sent over to the

Kenton in June, where I was captain. I was pretty green and still wet behind the ears, but I was the captain.

One winter in the 1940s I was on the *W.A. Shepard* working the Illinois River in the ice. There was a bad ice gorge in Bull Island cutoff. We had to double up with other boats in order to get the barges through the gorge. One boat would let its barges sit in the ice while it assisted another boat through the gorge. Once the barges were clear of the gorge, the boat with the barges would go on until it found a good solid tree to tie the barges off to. The assisting boat would go back down and pick up its barges and start up into the gorge. As soon as the other boat had its barges tied off, it would come back and assist the other boat through the gorge. It did not matter what the name of the company was, everyone helped each other to get through the gorges. If we hadn't helped each other, no one would have made it through.

During this time period the boats did not have a lot of horsepower. The M/V's *Horace Horton, Chicago Bridge, Mary Ellen* and another boat were all working together to get the barges through. Most of the boats did not have shortwave radios, so we'd get close to one another, take a megaphone and holler the message we wanted to pass on.

We also used a lot of whistle signals—one to stop, one to come ahead, two to back up, and so on. One day we'd been doing pretty well getting the various barges through the ice gorge. I had my barges through, had put them back together, and was pushing upriver. A short distance above Bull Island is a pretty sharp turn called Milliken Bend. I was unable to make the steer around the bend, so I had to knock out (uncouple from my barges) and take the light boat and break out a path in the ice for my tow.

A short way upriver from me was a southbound Socony Vacuum Oil Company boat with four empty petroleum barges. He was stopped because he could not push through the ice. I broke up the ice almost up to him and if he had lain still, everything would have been fine. However, while I was facing my boat up to my tow, the captain on the Socony Vacuum boat shoved his barges down into the hole I had made, almost to the head of my tow. I had to knock my boat out of tow again. With my light boat, I broke up a lot of ice and was able to work him around my barges in order to get him out of the way.

If the reader does not understand about river ice, maybe I can explain. Once the ice is broken up enough, a boat can steer through it fairly easily. However, it must get through before the ice knits (freezes) back together. When the temperature is around zero, ice freezes back together in a very short time.

Since river towboats push barges ahead of them and are fastened to the barges with large wire cables, we say the boat is "facing up" to the tow or barge. It takes a lot of work to wire a boat to a tow, and quite a bit time. After getting the Socony Vacuum boat out of the way, I pushed on up the river. We locked through the Marseilles lock and turned another boat, somewhere in the vicinity of Seneca or Morris, Illinois. By "turning another boat," I mean that I gave him my northbound loaded coal barges and took over his southbound empty barges.

When I came back downriver with my empty barges, the Socony Vacuum boat was still above the Bull Island cut and not doing so well. Some of the other boats were having the same trouble with the Socony Vacuum captain that I had experienced. As soon as they would make a hole in the ice, he would shove

M/V W.A. Shepard, *originally owned by the Kelly Barge Line towing on the Lower Mississippi River. Here the* Shepard *is towing coal, but when the barges were carrying baled cotton, it was necessary to add another pilot-house to the boat in order for the pilot to see over the bales.*

his barges down into it and get in the way. The ice gorge was getting worse. Finally the Socony Vacuum boat decided to drop two barges and try it with just the other two barges. It still didn't work, so we (the other four boats working the gorge) got our heads together and decided to push him out of the way. We told him we'd give him a boost, and he was all for it.

The M/Vs *Shepard, Horace Horton, Chicago Bridge,* and *Mary Ellen* faced up on the stern of the Socony Vacuum boat in a straight line, one behind the other. All together we had over 10,000 horsepower pushing on those two barges. When we were all set, with a toot of the whistle, we came ahead and away we went. The only difficulty was that we couldn't make the turn into the Bull Island cut. The ice behind Bull Island was very thick. The captain on the Socony Vacuum boat suddenly realized that we could not make the turn, so he started blowing a lot of whistles to get us to stop. We all had had enough of him, so we just kept shoving until the ice stopped us. When we came to a stop, the lead empty barge was sitting on top of the ice, completely out of the water, high and dry. We made a halfhearted show of trying to back it off the ice, but it didn't budge an inch. Then we left the captain to his own devices. Eventually he worked around and finally got one barge backed off. The outcome of the event was that he went on to St. Louis a couple of days later with three barges, leaving one barge sitting on top of the ice for about three weeks until the weather warmed and he returned the next time around. He pulled the same kind of shenanigans while trying to work through the ice gorge at Chillicothe, Illinois. Needless to say, he wasn't liked by very many of the other pilots or boat crews.

• • •

In the 1940s there was a man we called "Crazy Mike" who was first mate on the *W. A. Shepard.* On the last trip of the season out of the Upper Mississippi River, the *Shepard* had to pick up an empty barge at the Genoa power plant about eleven p.m. The temperature was around five to ten degrees, and the wind was blowing very hard. While running the barge around the head of the tow to put it in place in the tow, Mike was riding on the empty barge and the deckhand carrying the end of the line (rope) was on the main fleet of barges. They would check the barge down every so often so they could control its speed. The deckhand dropped his end of the line and away went the empty barge, with Crazy Mike aboard. The wind and current carried the barge down over a wing dam and into a slough. It floated into the slough about a thousand feet, where it was stopped by the ice, which was forming very rapidly.

The *Shepard* tied off its tow to a tree on the right descending bank and went back light boat to get the barge. It was unable to get over the wing dam, as the boat drew too much water. (The barge was only drawing eighteen inches.) The deck crew tried to carry a line down to the barge with a yawl with no outboard motor, only oars. It was only about a thousand feet away, but the ice was being formed so fast they couldn't even get close to the empty barge. The *W. A. Shepard* went light boat back up to Lock No. 8. The lockmen called around and located a fisherman who had a motorboat, but his engine was partially torn down for the winter. The chief engineer from the *Shepard* helped the fisherman put his engine back together and put his boat back into the river.

The fisherman's boat had enough power to push through the ice even though the river was making ice very fast. With the help of the motorboat, the crew finally got a line down to the barge, and with the aid of the capstan on the *Shepard*, the crew pulled the barge back out of the slough and put it in tow. Mike had been on the barge all this time and nearly froze to death. He had crawled down into a hatch hole to get out of the wind, but had no matches to build a fire. Since then, I've always called this slough "Crazy Mike Slough."

• • •

In late 1937, I went to St. Louis and obtained a tankerman's certificate. We were going to start towing petroleum barges into Chicago and Blue Island, Illinois, for the John I. Hay Company. The law required the towing boat to have a certified tankerman aboard at all times.

On September 12, 1938, after passing the test, I became "Licensed as Operator of Motor Vessels, Any Waters" by the Steamboat Inspection Service, Department of Commerce. Captain George B. Gordon and David W. Layfield were the local inspectors of the Steamboat Inspection Service.

On October 29th, 1939, I was issued a first-class pilot license on the Illinois River from Havana, Illinois, to Joliet, Illinois. It was issued by the Steamboat Inspection Service, at this time under the Department of Commerce. Captain George Gordon and Captain "Stogie" White were the inspectors. In 1940 the Steamboat Inspection Service was taken over by the United States Coast Guard.

The requirements when I received my first class pilot's license were that you had to have served on a boat for thirty-six months, pass a written examination covering rules of the road, boat construction techniques, number of lifeboats required, fire fighting equipment, and first aid and medical safety aboard a boat (given by the United States Public Health Service and based on their book *Ship's Medicine Chest and First Aid at Sea*).

After the written examination, you had to draw a freehand chart (map) of the section of the river you wished to be licensed for. The chart had to show all navigation lights with name and mileage, all buoys, all creeks emptying into the river, all islands and sandbars with their names, all bridges with their horizontal and vertical clearances, all power lines with their heights, and the names of towns and cities. It also helped to note the depth of the water at certain locations. It was a very through examination!

If you passed everything, you were issued a license that was good for five years. If you later wished to extend your license to more sections of the river, you had to have made ten round trips over the section you wished to draw and then draw a chart of that section.

To obtain a master's license, you had to obtain a pilot's license and serve one year on a boat, and then you were given a much more detailed written examination covering the subjects you had been tested on for the pilot's license. I went to the Chicago office of the United States Coast Guard to take the test for my master's license. (This was when the Inspection Service was changing over to the Coast Guard from the Department of Commerce.) They handed me a test for a Great Lakes master license. I told them I wanted a river master's license. I was told that the Great Lakes exam was the only one they had; it was that or nothing. So I wrote that test. I was lucky though, for I had studied the Great Lakes rules and regulations books thoroughly and even though the test had a lot of questions about passenger vessels, I was able to pass it successfully.

I was on the *W. A. Shepard* most of the fall and through December, 1940. A couple of times I was shifted to the *Kenton* or *Kosmos* running in the Chicago Sanitary Canal, between Joliet and Chicago. The United States Corps of Engineers maintained the navigation lights and buoys at this time. Starting in November, they tried to have all the buoys in the river and float lights in Peoria Lake out of the river and lake by November 15 and did not put them back until the middle of April. But we ran all winter anyway, without too much difficulty. We simply had to learn the river and remember where the good water was.

In early January of 1940, the Central Barge Company decid-

On this page and the next two are examples of hand-drawn charts similar to the one required for the pilot's test.

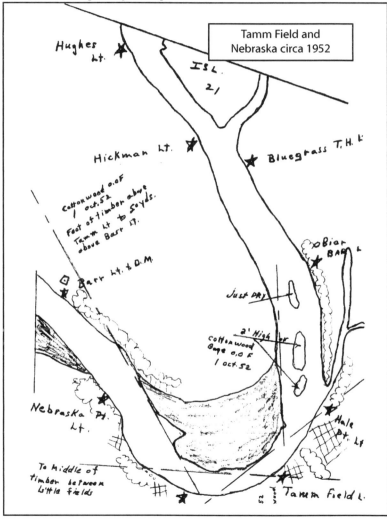

ed to tie the boats up, as the ice was really heavy. We tied the *Shepard* up at Henry, Illinois, and I was sent home to Ottawa, Illinois. I was only home one night. Early the next morning the telephone rang and it was the dispatcher telling

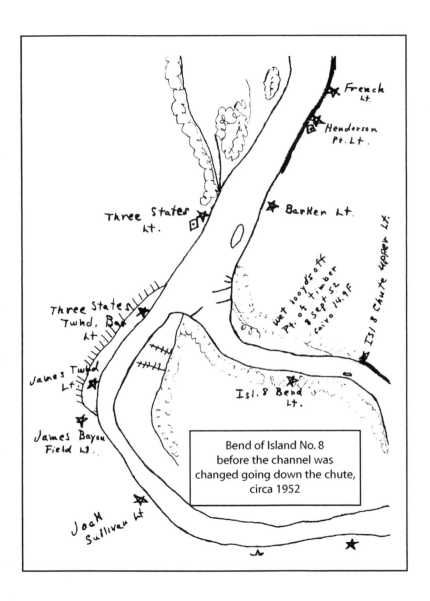

Bend of Island No. 8 before the channel was changed going down the chute, circa 1952

me I was to go to Marmet, West Virginia, and get on the M/V
Laura H, a 120-horsepower sternwheel boat.

I took a train to Charleston, West Virginia, and a taxi or bus
to Marmet, a small coal mining town on the Kanawha River.

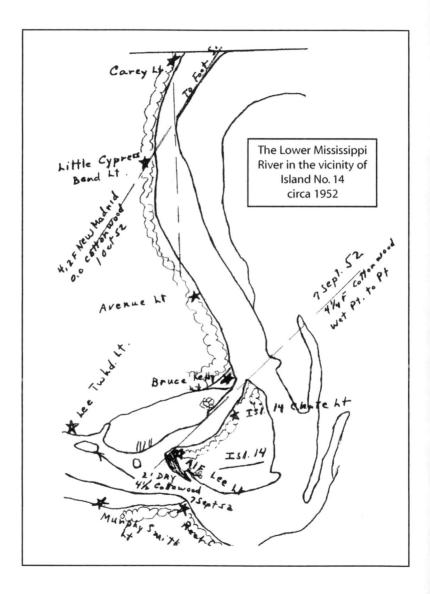

The Lower Mississippi
River in the vicinity of
Island No. 14
circa 1952

CHAPTER 7

The boat only ran in daylight, towing coal from a coal mine tipple located about ten miles upriver to a dock in Marmet. The quarters on the *Laura H* were not so good, so I found a room in town not too far from the dock where we tied up at night.

My best memory of this period was taking a girl to Charleston to see *Gone with the Wind*. She worked in the restaurant in Marmet where I ate a lot of my meals. She only lived about twenty miles or so away, back up in a hollow, but she had no idea how to get there from Marmet. Her brother had brought her into town and she lived with the woman who ran the restaurant.

• • •

I was on the *Laura H* for six weeks and was relieved by Captain George Howe. I went back to Joliet, Illinois, and worked mostly on the *W. A. Shepard*. Every so often I would have to make a few trips on either the *Kosmos* or *Kenton*.

The *Kosmos* and *Kenton* did not have hydraulic pilothouses at this time, so seeing over empty barges was very difficult and involved a lot of guesswork. A pilot named Joe knocked the pilothouse off the *Kosmos* hitting a low bridge in Chicago. Some of the steel under the bridges was arched and a boat passing under the bridge had to be fairly well centered to clear everything and Joe wasn't. The company maintenance crew at the Joliet landing built the pilothouse halfway back. They put a roof on, and a door, but no windows. The boat was needed to keep the coal barges moving to the Commonwealth Edison Power plants in Chicago, so we ran with an open-air pilothouse. Since it was nice spring weather with a minimum of rain, it wasn't really bad; the pilots just got a lot of fresh air.

After several weeks on the *Kosmos*, I was transferred to the *Sylvia T* running between Joliet and Havana, Illinois.

M/V Laura H.
PHOTO BY AUTHOR

*Running in ice on the
Kanawha River.*
PHOTO BY AUTHOR

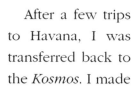

After a few trips to Havana, I was transferred back to the *Kosmos*. I made one trip into Chicago and back. When I returned to Joliet after that first trip, the port engineer, Bill Trierweiler, asked me how I liked being able to see over the empty barges. While I was on the *Sylvia T,* they had installed a hydraulic pilothouse on the *Kosmos*. A hydraulic pilothouse is mounted on a ram to raise it so the pilot can see over the empty barges and lower it to clear low bridges.

I told him I couldn't say, he'd have to see for himself. We went out to the boat and I demonstrated that when I stood up straight between the steering levers my fingertips didn't quite reach them—I had to bend over to reach them. He laughed, because he and Captain Chuck Partridge, both short men, had figured for some time and decided the levers were just the right height. Needless to say, they raised them before we left on the next trip. (Note: On most riverboats with power steering there is not a pilot wheel. The old-time boats did have a pilot wheel and it was connected directly to the rudders by wire rope. There also was a foot brake that the pilot used to keep the wheel from turning, especially when the boat was backing and throwing a lot of water against the rudders. With power steering there are usually two levers, one on either side of where the pilot stands. These levers are connected to a valve that operates a hydraulic ram, which is connected to the rudders.)

Another change was made on the *Kosmos* while I worked on another boat: a second searchlight was installed. After I returned from my first trip into Chicago on the *Kosmos*, Bill asked me how I enjoyed having two searchlights. I asked him why they had bothered to install a second one since we could only use one at a time. He wanted to know why we could only use one—the company had added another electric generator to handle the second searchlight. I told him I didn't know, but the chief engineer had informed me that he only had enough power for one. Bill told me to get the engineer over to the office, right now! When questioned, the engineer said, "Two generators use too much gasoline." Bill told him that the company would make the judgment on the gasoline, and he, as chief engineer, was to keep both generators running every night. From then on the pilots could use two searchlights whenever they wished.

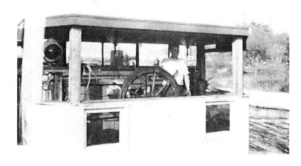

Open-air pilot-house on the Kosmos.

PHOTO BY AUTHOR

8 The Upper Mississippi River

In April the company had the *W. A. Shepard* running in the coal trade between Alton, Illinois, and St. Paul, Minnesota. I was sent as steersman to the *Alexander Mackenzie*, a new steamboat the Central Barge Company had built in 1939 at the Marietta Manufacturing Company shipyard in Point Pleasant, West Virginia. It was a sternwheel, coal-burning boat of 1600 horsepower that carried a crew of twenty-five. The *Mackenzie*, her sister boat the Str. *Jason* and the Str. *Jack Rathbone* were the last three sternwheel steam towboats ever built.

Harry Morse was captain and Carl Hall was chief engineer. I steered on the *Mackenzie* for twenty-three days. We only got up to Savanna, Illinois, mile 536 on the Upper Mississippi River, where we turned a boat, and south to President Island below Memphis, Tennessee, to turn the Str. *America* of the American Barge Line.

Then I was transferred to the *W. A. Shepard*. Captain L. J. Sullivan was the master-pilot and I was the pilot. We ran between Cairo, Illinois, and St. Paul, Minnesota, until the close of the navigation season in the fall.

Str. Alexander Mackenzie. PHOTO BY BOAT PHOTO MUSEUM, MARYVILLE, ILLINOIS

During this period, the company started to shift deckhands and mates around so they would have experience on various types of boats. Every time a man who had been on the *Shepard* would come aboard the *Mackenzie*, the captain would question him, wanting to know how many times the *Shepard* had been aground or messed up running the bridges. We were lucky and ran the whole season without a grounding or bad mishap. I can't say the same for the *Mackenzie*.

On the *Shepard*, every so often we made a trip to Cairo and sometimes up the Ohio River to Smithland, Kentucky, where we got barges that were being brought down the Cumberland River by a towboat from Nashville, Tennessee. On one trip, while we were waiting at Smithland for the barges to arrive, some of the crew went to town to get some bootleg whiskey. (Smithland was in a dry county.) The men walked to the bootlegger's house and found his wife hanging her washing on the clothesline in the side yard. She told the crew that they didn't have any whiskey, explaining, "The old —— drank it all up, and there he lays." He was sleeping it off on the ground in the backyard.

During the first week of November in 1940, I got off the

Strs. Alexander Mackenzie *and* America. *One knew there was a coal-burning steamboat coming, even around a bend, because of the black smoke.*

Shepard at Clarksville, Missouri, at Lock No. 24 and caught a C. B. & Q train to Red Wing, Minnesota, to get on the *Sylvia T.* I boarded the *Sylvia T* at the Red Wing riverfront around three a.m. The temperature was fifty-nine degrees at six a.m. and it was raining. The company rule was that we had to log the weather conditions every six hours in the logbook. We went into Minneapolis to wait for some grain barges to be loaded. The morning of November 11 it was raining, but still very warm. I went off watch and to bed. When I awoke about ten a.m., it was snowing very hard and the temperature was dropping rapidly. Shortly after noon, several of the crew decided we'd better find some warmer clothes. All we had was light summer clothing since none of the crew had been up north in the wintertime.

I tried to phone for a taxi from the wharf office. The taxi operator simply said, "No cabs available," and hung up. A short time later I called again and they wouldn't even answer the phone. About this time a truck driver came into the wharf office and was stamping the snow off his boots. As I hung up the phone I said to my crewmates, "We'll just go up and catch a streetcar." The truck driver informed us that the storm was a full-blown blizzard, and not a streetcar or taxi was mov-

M/V Sylvia T
at Minneapolis,
Minnesota, on
Armistice Day,
1940.

PHOTO BY AUTHOR

ing anywhere in the Twin Cities. The snow was already too deep for traffic to move. This was about one p.m.

The snow was still falling very heavily. We decided to walk into town and try to find a clothing store that was open. On our way up the street, we stopped and pushed a couple of autos away from the curb so they could get going. It was Armistice Day and a lot of the stores were closed, but luckily we found one that was open. We purchased some warmer work pants, heavy jackets and gloves. Murf, one of the deckhands, saw a suit that he liked and bought it. Of course, it had to have some tailoring work done on it. The rest of us didn't want to wait, so we went back to the boat. Murf didn't get back to the boat that night.

The next morning the temperature was five degrees below zero and the river was frozen over solid. There was three feet of snow on the ground. We didn't know where Murf was, so some of us got off the boat onto the dock and looked up and down the wharf to see if he could have fallen into the river, but there were no signs of anyone walking off the dock and there were no holes in the ice.

Captain Red Steele had gone to Chicago to attend a court trial as soon as we arrived in Minneapolis, and I was left in

M/V Sylvia T *as a new boat.*

charge as master. I was just about to the point of calling the office and reporting a man missing when Murf showed up. He told us that when his suit was finished, it was late and dark. He went into a bar near the clothing store and an old lady told him the way the weather was he'd better not try to get back to the boat. She offered him a bed to sleep in. Her apartment was right next door to the tavern, so Murf stayed in town. We finally got our six barges together and started down the river, breaking ice. It was cold, below zero at night and only moving up to the single digits during the day.

Captain A. C. Ingersoll, Jr. joined us as master, for which I was glad. We fought ice all the way down the river, adding more loaded barges on the way. Finally, at Keokuk, Iowa, we had twelve grain loads in tow. The only way I made the old Quincy railroad bridge was by doing what we call rough-locking the tow down the bank. In other words, backing the tow into the bank and letting it slide down the shore to slow it down enough so I could safely get through the bridge. We did somehow get the tow to Alton safely by the grace of God.

M/V Wheelock Whitney.

That storm was later known at the Armistice Day Storm of 1940. We didn't know it at the time, but that Armistice Day forty duck hunters were frozen to death between Locks No. 5 and No. 5-A, a distance of ten miles. They had gone out that morning dressed for mild weather and the blizzard hit about noon. The wind got up to sixty miles per hour and made the water so rough that their small boats would have been swamped if they had tried to get out into the river.

Captain Bob Richtman was at home during the storm. He attended a dance that evening at the American Legion in Fountain City, Wisconsin, the home port of the United States Corps of Engineers maintenance fleet for the St. Paul District. When the people at the dance heard gunshots coming from the bottoms, they knew the hunters were in trouble. There were no boats large enough to handle the furious wind and rough water except the Corps of Engineers' boats, but all of the Corps of Engineers boat operators were gone for the weekend. Bob tried to get permission to run one of the Corps boats, but could not get it because he didn't work for the government. He might have been able to save some of those

M/V Sarah McDonald.

poor souls—the Richtman boys were born and raised in Fountain City and knew those river bottoms like the palms of their hands.

• • •

During the summer of 1941, I spent some more time on the *Sylvia T* and was also on the *W. A. Shepard* when the company decided to change her name to *Wheelock Whitney*. I painted the new name on her name boards while steering up the river.

I also spent ten days or so on the M/V *Sarah McDonald*, about 250 horsepower with a sternwheel and no monkey rudders (small rudders behind the paddlewheel).

The *Sarah McDonald* would not do anything on the Illinois River. She'd take a run toward the shore and we'd have to back her in order throw water against the rudders to make her kick her stern around and straighten up. This would make us lose all our headway. The pilot wheel had a foot brake, and you had to step on the brake hard once you started to back up, because when the water hit the rudders it would spin the pilot wheel and throw you out of the pilothouse if you tried to hold onto it without the brake on. The company got rid of the *Sarah McDonald* in a hurry. I think they only had her about a month.

• • •

I joined the *Alexander Mackenzie* at Winona, Minnesota, at the end of October 1941, just after completing my pilot license extension on the Upper Mississippi River. At the start of December, we went up the Illinois River to enter the Commonwealth Edison coal trade between Havana and Joliet. Once the *Mackenzie* entered the Illinois River at Grafton, there was a change in the pilothouse furniture. Two large wicker rocking chairs were removed so the pilot wouldn't have anything to stumble over when he wanted to run outside to watch his stern, for the boat was big to be running up a small crooked river.

I was running master and Captain Bruce Freeburg was my pilot. I was assisting Bruce into the Marseilles lock when the radio came on with the news that the Japanese had bombed Pearl Harbor. The upper guide wall at the Marseilles lock was being rebuilt at this time and the lock was very tricky to enter. When we came back northbound a couple of days later from Havana, the lockmen were all wearing sidearms or carrying rifles or shotguns and the situation around the locks had changed drastically because of the war. I got off at Starved Rock Lock northbound to visit my folks, who lived in Ottawa. They took me back to the Marseilles lock to catch the boat. The *Mackenzie* was lying at the lower lock wall waiting to lock. I went down through the weeds as usual to get on the boat. I heard my Dad shout a couple of times, "Don't you shoot that boy." One of the lockmen had a bead on me and was going to shoot. I sure didn't do that again. Everyone was on edge the first few days after the Pearl Harbor attack. All the railroad bridges and major electric highline crossings had armed guards posted on them almost immediately. Guard shacks were built in the highline towers to house the guards.

• • •

During the winter of 1941-1942, I was on the *Mackenzie* standing the afterwatch as we came down through Peoria Lake. At about one a.m., I had an urgent need to go to the bathroom, so I told the mate, Dusty Rhoads, to steer for me while I went downstairs. I told him to keep her headed on a red beer sign until I got back. When I came back we were headed on a red light, but I realized it was not the right one. I asked Dusty if he had lost the light. He told me he had lost it but found it again. What had happened was that at one a.m. the tavern had closed and turned off the beer sign. But far around to the right, at Mossville, Illinois, there was a tavern that stayed open most of the night. Dusty was headed on a red beer sign, but it was the wrong beer sign, so we were far out of the channel and headed in the wrong direction.

The weather was very hazy and we couldn't see anything. I knew what direction the wind was coming from, so after we got the boat stopped, I knew we were headed straight into the shore. The area we were in had been known as the cabbage patch before the dam at Peoria raised the water level because truck farmers raised vegetables there. Very slowly, I got the boat headed in what I thought was the right direction and slowly pushed in that direction, with the deck crew using a lead line to give me water depth. I was lucky enough to get back into the channel without going aground. The river stage this night was a little above normal, which was lucky for us.

I had another similar experience on the Upper Mississippi River in Lake Pepin. I was southbound on the *W. A. Shepard* with a tow of empty barges. I had to go to the bathroom about ten p.m. and told the second mate, Shorty Halverson, to keep her headed on a red light on the block signal on the railroad tracks that ran down the Minnesota shore. When I came back we were headed on a red light, all right, but straight into the bank! I just had time to get us turned in the right direction before we would have hit the bank head on. I found out later that right after I left the pilothouse, the train going down the track had left the block, so the light switched to green. So much for using trains signals to give steering directions.

During this time I was shifted from the *Mackenzie* to the *Shepard* to the *Sylvia T* several times, usually running master on whichever boat I was moved to.

I was working the Upper Mississippi River during the navigation season, usually from March to the first of December, and the Illinois River during the winter months. In 1941, I met a very beautiful red-headed girl from Indiana who was attending Indiana State College. Ernestine was a friend of my sister, Barbara, who was also attending Indiana State College. We were married on March 22, 1942, and moved to an apartment in Ottawa, Illinois. We lived in Ottawa for three years, then purchased a home in Field Hills, a subdivision in north Ottawa.

In 1946, my wife and I bought a forty-acre farm near Cory, Indiana, and moved there when my son Steve was six weeks old. Grandfather Stevenson thought Ottawa, Illinois, was too far away for his grandson. The farm we bought was only two miles away from the Stevenson farm where Ernestine was born. But that is another story.

9 *The Lower Mississippi River*

In July, the company sent me to the *Alexander Mackenzie*, which was running on the Ohio and Lower Mississippi Rivers. She was towing oil from the Pipe Line Project Five dock at Helena, Arkansas, to North Bend, Ohio. The government had required the company to convert eight new coal barges into oil barges. Three of the barges had just been built and had not yet been delivered. They were simply moved to another shipyard to be converted into oil tank barges. The other five new barges had made one trip to St. Paul loaded with coal. From there they were taken to a shipyard where they were converted into tank barges by putting in cross bulkheads and using the steel from rolltop covers to make the tops for the barges. Because of the war, steel was in short supply and nothing was wasted. The German U-boats were sinking our tankers off the East Coast at a rapid rate and the Big Inch pipeline had not been completed. Everything that could move a few barrels of oil was pressed into service. The Defense Plant Corporation built some oil barges using steel framing with wood for the tops, sides and bottom, but they did not work well and were soon abandoned.

At Dubuque, Iowa, on the Upper Mississippi River, I got off the *W. A. Shepard* with orders to go to the *Alexander Mackenzie*. I took a train to Chicago and met Captain Connie Ingersoll at the Central Barge Company office. He and I took a Pennsylvania Railroad train to Louisville, Kentucky. On arrival we called Lock No. 41 and discovered that the boat had already locked through and gone on south. We saw on the train board that there was a train leaving shortly for Brandenburg, Kentucky. Connie said, "Oh, we'll catch her there," so we hopped on it. Neither of us knew a thing about the countryside and when we arrived at Brandenburg about midnight, the conductor asked, "You boys know where you're getting off?" We replied, "Yes, Brandenburg." He said he just wanted to be sure.

We got off with an old couple and one other man who immediately got into a car and took off. Someone met the old couple and they left in another car. The train departed. It was pitch black except for one bare lightbulb hanging outside a small station building a couple of hundred feet away. We walked over to the station and saw a drunk leaning against the building. We asked him where the town was. He pointed and sheepishly said, "Thataway." We asked about a taxi and as he rubbed his whiskers he replied, "That's where the rub comes in—they ain't none." We picked up our luggage and started to hike down a road that eventually led through town to the riverbank.

The long walk made us understand why the conductor had questioned us about getting off at Brandenburg. Our suitcases had become quite heavy by the time we arrived at the riverbank around four a.m. About daybreak the *Mackenzie* came around Tobacco Bend. We lit a newspaper and frantically waved it to attract the boat's attention. The *Mackenzie* sent a yawl in and picked us up. Captain Don "Red" Steel was master. We made a trip to Helena, Arkansas, where we loaded the barges with oil, and returned to North Bend, Ohio.

One of the trip-pilots was Captain "Available," called that because he was not much of a pilot and companies only hired him when they were short of a pilot and had to have a licensed pilot. I stood watch with him the first morning below Cairo, Illinois, where he had joined us. He was on watch and coming down into a sharp bend called Happy Valley. I watched him as long as I could stand it and finally said, "Captain, if you don't back up you're going to hit the bank." He immediately backed away from the steering levers and said, "Here, you take her—you know more about this boat than I do." The same thing happened later in the morning at Forked Deer, where there was also a sharp bend. When Captain Steel ambled into the pilothouse a little later, I took him aside and told him what had happened. He said, "My God, don't let him steer—you're supposed to be doing the work. He's just on here for his license."

The next trip, coming back down the river, Captain Steel got a burr under his saddle and quit, and I inherited the master's job on the *Mackenzie*. We ran in the Helena, Arkansas, to North Bend, Ohio, trade for a year or so, then started to tow out of Marrero, Louisiana, across the river from New Orleans. As soon as I had made enough trips over a stretch of river, I'd go to the Coast Guard office and take the license examination. And as soon as I received a license for a stretch of river, I'd start standing the master pilot's watch. I worked a lot of extra hours both as master and pilot and did most of the landing work. A lot of the trip-pilots we had were not very skilled, especially when it came to handling the light boat. The boat would flip around if you tried to back her down very far without a barge on her head to steady her up.

Whenever Captain "Available" was on duty, I was sure to have trouble. He wouldn't crowd the willows or sandbars to miss the current and if he did attempt it, he'd end up aground and I'd have to get up and get us off the ground. On one trip, he was standing a watch and grounded the tow. It took several hours to get it off the ground and put it back together. Tows usually broke apart on grounding, and sometimes we had to work one barge at a time off the ground. I ended up handling the boat *and* working down on deck because our deck crew was young and very inexperienced—anything unusual they had to be shown.

During the grounding incident, I'd had a lot of exercise running up and down the stairs from the main deck to the pilothouse and back, so after getting the boat underway, I went to my room to clean up. I was in the shower, all soaped up, when I felt the boat touch bottom again. I quickly rinsed off and rushed to the pilothouse. Sure enough, we were aground again. It took another twelve hours to get going. At least I did get the soap rinsed off before I felt us ground a third time. Again it took ten or twelve hours before we were going again. I told Captain "Available," in no uncertain terms, to hold her out in the river until I got some sleep. His comment was, "She won't make any time." I told him I didn't care, but he'd better not ground her again until I rested. I think I would have thrown him overboard if he had grounded again. I was completely worn out after being up for thirty-six or more hours.

• • •

Pilots were in very short supply due to the war effort. The Defense Plant Corporation had built twenty-one 2000-horsepower steamboats and numerous tugs and leased them to various barge lines to run. The Central Barge Company

DPC towboat, originally Str. Gona, *one of twenty-one boats built by the Defense Plant Corporation during World War II.*

chartered the DPC-50, DPC-67 and DPC-68. They were diesel-powered, 750-horsepower, single-screw, regular harbor tugs and were used to push coal barges from Havana to Joliet on the Illinois River.

• • •

While on the *Alexander Mackenzie* on the Lower Mississippi River, I received a letter from my wife wanting to know what was happening on the Illinois River. She had seen a tow going downriver at Ottawa—two tugs faced up to eight empty barges with three barges on one side, three barges on the other side, and two barges in the middle. One tug was faced up toward the barges going downstream and the other, on the head end, was facing upstream.

The reason for this strange tow arrangement was that the tug crews had found out that with a tug on either end they could keep the tow moving when the wind blew, and it does blow on the Illinois River. Chicago is known as the Windy City for a good reason. When the wind blew, one boat pushed down the river and the other came ahead when needed to help the pushing tug steer. I imagine it was scary at times on the tug that was being pushed backwards down the river, but they did get the job done. Rusty Mitchell, who worked on one of these setups, told me that whenever he was on boat being pushed he wouldn't sleep there but on the boat doing the pushing. I didn't get a chance to enjoy working on the DPC tugs, thank goodness.

EMPTY BARGE		EMPTY BARGE		EMPTY BARGE	
DPC TUG	EMPTY BARGE		EMPTY BARGE		DPC TUG
EMPTY BARGE		EMPTY BARGE		EMPTY BARGE	

Diagram of DPC tugs taking empty barges down the Illinois when the wind was blowing during World War II.

• • •

The Company sent Captain Orville "Dusty" Rhoads to learn the Lower Mississippi River and the Ohio River. Eventually Captain Truman Mayfield took a regular pilot job on the *Mackenzie,* for which I was thankful. We had various trip-pilots and some were fair and some so-so. We always had eight loads and two fuel flats (barges). For a while we had two Gulf Oil Company barges, which were extra. After several trips the company decided that the extra barges were not paying off, so we did away with them. The *Mackenzie* burned fifty tons of coal every twenty-four hours in open river conditions. (Open river conditions means that there was enough water so the Corps of Engineers could lower the dams and we didn't have to lock.) We carried two fuel barges (175 feet by 26 feet by 11 feet) and always picked up the loaded fuel barges at Cincinnati. We used the coal from one of the barges on our way south. That barge would be dropped at Bob Petty's fleet at Cairo or Warner & Tamble's fleet at Memphis to be picked up on our northbound trip. We could then go south with a full barge of fuel.

The *Alexander Mackenzie* had a boom and bucket arrangement to move the coal aboard the boat. The boat could hold only about 150 tons of coal in her fuel bunkers, so we had to load coal every day. On several occasions during the time I was aboard we'd have a grounding while we were coaling and tear a boom down, so we always carried an extra boom. The crew could change the boom very quickly and we never had to use the "Irish buggies" (wheelbarrows) that we carried in the hold in case of an emergency.

On one trip we picked up a fuel barge loaded with coal from Caseyville, Kentucky. Caseyville coal was the bane of riverboat firemen. It didn't burn well and made unbelievable clinkers. A fireman would use a slice bar (a long steel bar used to break clinkers into smaller pieces) to pick up the whole firebox because it was one huge clinker. He'd have to break the clinker into pieces to remove it from the firebox. One load of Caseyville coal was all we got because we couldn't keep steam pressure up with it.

Later on, the War Production Board in Washington, D.C., decided that we should burn a mixture of sixty percent good coal and forty percent fines (very small pieces of coal, much of which is coal dust). The fines would go through the firebox and exhaust out the stacks without even being burned—hardly scorched, as a matter of fact.

When we came to a hard place to shove through on the Lower Mississippi River, we were unable to keep the steam pressure up and had to tie off some of our barges and double-trip through the hard place.

After my many complaints about the coal, a man from the War Production Board got on the boat when we were a couple of days out of Cincinnati. He fired the boat himself to see how the coal was burning. We were in easy pool water in the Ohio River so the engineers did not have to work the boat very hard and we made good time. When we arrived at our destination, the oil terminal at North Bend, Ohio, I went to the telephone in the pumphouse shanty office on the hill. Among other topics, I talked to the office regarding what kind of coal our next fuel barges were loaded with. I was told it would be sixty percent good coal and forty percent fines. I didn't know the War Production man was nearby listening to me and really didn't care. I blew my top and spouted off to my port engineer. After I hung up, the War Production man said to me, "When I came up the hill, I was ready to tell Washington that your coal was OK, but after listening to you just now, I've changed my mind. Captain, I can guarantee that you will get good coal from now on." He was good to his word and we got good coal after that, with no fines!

The *Mackenzie* put out lots of smoke and cinders. The lockmen's wives who lived on the lock reservations hated us because of this, and with good reason. One trip, at Lock No. 6, Trempealeau, Wisconsin, we came up to the lock just after the lockmaster's wife had hung her washing out to dry. She had left for town not knowing the *Mackenzie* was in the vicinity. She returned just as we were finishing locking, and she was one upset woman. The wind was blowing our smoke and cinders right over her laundry and she had to rewash everything. At that time the boats had no radios, so the lockmen didn't know where we were or when we would arrive until we showed up and whistled for the lock. We didn't even have a tow public address system with speakers on the barges until sometime in 1944 or 1945.

● ● ●

During World War II, I was on the *Alexander Mackenzie* northbound at Vicksburg, Mississippi. I usually made the yawl play (took a rowboat) to the wharf barge to pick up mail myself. Our outboard motor was broken and because of the war we were unable to get repair parts, so we used the oars to propel the yawl, but none of the crew had any experience rowing a yawl in strong current. When we made the yawl play, the deck crew put the yawl in the water and pulled it out to the head of the tow, and when the pilot was ready for the yawl to go he would give a short toot on the whistle. One day I told the first mate, Heavy Johnson, to take a deckhand named Red and make the yawl play to get the mail. I reminded him to wait for the pilot to give him a whistle.

I went down and ate dinner, and as I was coming up the stairs to the pilothouse, I heard the pilot cussing a blue streak. Heavy had turned loose on his own, down much too low. (When making a yawl play in strong current, you must start above your landing place to allow for the current carrying you downstream while you are rowing across to the landing spot.) There's a lot of very fast current down the Vicksburg shore. I ran up to the pilothouse in time to see the Red fanning the oars like a windmill and Heavy sitting in the stern with his arms folded like Captain Bligh of the *Bounty*. They barely made it over to the wharf barge and caught the last place where there was anything to grab hold of. Heavy couldn't get out of the yawl because the deck of the wharf barge was too high, so he boosted Red up onto the wharf to get the mail. We waited and waited and finally, after about two hours, Red showed up. About the same time, a small tug emerged from the Yazoo River mouth. I hailed the tug pilot and asked if he would pick up my yawl at the wharf barge and bring it out

Str. Alexander Mackenzie *leaving Lock No. 24, Clarksville, Missouri at 2:25 p.m., November 10, 1941 bound for the Twin Cities with fourteen loads of coal and a fuel flat, a total of 14,303 tons, upstream on open river.*   COURTESY CENTRAL BARGE COMPANY

to me, which he did. The mate, Heavy Johnson, came to the pilothouse and said, "No mail," and left. I knew I had mail there and the chief engineer was supposed to have some. I thought something was wrong, so I called Red up to the pilot-house and asked him who was in the office, since it was Saturday. He replied, "A watchman, and that was all."

The mail was kept in a box about twelve feet long, twelve inches wide and twelve inches deep; the mail from many boats was thrown in together, totaling several hundred pieces. I asked Red who checked the mail. He said, "Me and the watchman." I said Red, you can't even write your own name and I doubt if the watchman can read or write either." Red said, "I couldn't let that black man [he used the n–word] know that I couldn't read or write." So the two had gone through the whole pile of mail handing pieces from one to the other, neither knowing what they were looking for. Needless to say, the mate hid out from the chief engineer for several days. I was not very happy either. We did pick up our mail on the next trip northbound through Vicksburg.

• • •

I was on the *Alexander McKenzie* northbound on the Ohio River during World War II. We had the usual tow of eight oil barges plus two Gulf Oil Company barges and the Str. *Minnesota* in tow. (The *Minnesota* was a dead boat; she was cooled down and had no crew aboard.) The only way we could make up the tow was with the *Minnesota* beside two oil barges; we ended up, with our tow, around 107 feet wide. One Sunday morning we came up to old Lock No. 41 and locked through without any difficulty, but above the lock several southbound boats had arrived while we were locking and they piled down into the Portland Canal. At this time the canal was only 200 feet wide between the concrete walls on both sides of the canal and the walls extended all the way from the lock to above the Pennsylvania Railroad bridge. We shoved out of the lock but were unable to squeeze by the other tows above the lock, as they were 105 feet wide. We couldn't narrow our tow because of the *Minnesota*, and the other boats were not very willing to narrow their tows. Meanwhile more boats were piling into the canal. Most boats didn't have radios, so communication was practically nonexistent. Finally there were seventeen towboats and ninety-seven barges crammed into the Portland Canal. Most were steamboats with empty petroleum barges in tow.

The Army Colonel in Charge of the Louisville District of the Corps of Engineers was driving up and down the road beside the canal, evidently very worried but not knowing what to do. One could have walked from the head of the canal to Lock No. 41 without stepping on land. With so many highly explo-

Str. Minnesota *was originally owned by the Doctors Mayo of Rochester, Minnesota and used as a pleasure boat. She was later sold to the St. Paul District Corps of Engineers and used as a survey boat and as a towboat moving quarter boats and rock barges. The Central Barge Company then acquired her, used her unsuccessfully, and she ended up as a landing and fleet barge at Cairo and, later, New Orleans.*   COURTESY CENTRAL BARGE CO.

sive empty petroleum barges and steamboats with open flames heating the boilers, I was worried about a fire or explosion.

By late Sunday night we got straightened out and proceeded up the river. As a result of that situation, the Corps of Engineers installed STOP and GO lights at the Eighteenth Street bridge. No southbound tow could come into the Portland Canal until it was given a green light. The lockmen at Lock No. 41 controlled the light, and it worked out very well. The Eighteenth Street Bridge has since been removed.

• • •

The deckhands were working in the paddlewheel tightening stirrups, bolts, etc. at North Bend, Ohio, while we were waiting to unload our cargo of oil. The paddlewheel was supposed to be blocked so it could not roll, but for some reason it rolled. The deckhands all got out safely, but the tools they were using fell into the river. We made another trip south, and when we came back into North Bend about three weeks later the river had fallen enough so the crew could go down and hunt in the weeds until they recovered all of our tools.

The same thing happened while we were tied up in a fog at the lower end of President Island below Memphis, except that we didn't recover our tools later—they were gone. I had just gone back to check on what was going on with the paddlewheel. The crew did not have a life ring on the fantail, where it would be handy, so I sent a man to get one. While he was gone, the striker in the engine room shifted a valve, which caused the paddlewheel to roll. Two deckhands went into the river. One grabbed a monkey rudder and one went floating down the river. When the man returned with the life ring, I threw it to the one who was floating away. It landed a foot or so from him, but he couldn't reach it. I hollered, asking him if he could make it. He said he didn't think he could. I pulled off my jacket and shirt, dove into the river and got hold of him and the life ring. We were floating down the river with the strong current. The chief engineer, who had rushed out to the fantail when the paddlewheel rolled, quickly put the yawl in the water, and two deckhands jumped into it and came down the river to get us.

When they got to us, they pulled the deckhand into the yawl and then pulled me in without much help on my part— I was so cold that my muscles would not work. This was in December and the water was probably between thirty-five and forty degrees and mighty cold, to say the least. We eventually got back to the boat and thawed out. That was enough December swimming for me. I wouldn't make a good polar bear.

10 A Bad Grounding

In 1945, the *Alexander Mackenzie* was northbound on the Lower Mississippi River with eight barges of oil and one fuel flat barge. We ran aground abreast of the mouth of the White River about two a.m. The Mississippi River was falling very fast. We had been running in a fog for about three days, one of those fogs that hangs just above the smokestacks. Suddenly the fog dropped down like a blanket over the pilothouse, shutting the pilot completely out. He was in a crossing just below Terreen Landing, Mississippi, and had no choice but to try to keep the tow straight with the current. There was a cross current that carried him sideways down onto the head of a sandbar. I was awakened, and I dressed and walked out on the barges to see how badly we were aground. A deckhand used a sounding pole to check the depth of water around the barges. I hollered to the pilot to stop the paddlewheel and lie still. We knocked off some of the wires between the barges and tried to move one or two barges but couldn't shake even one—they were all hard aground.

The deckhand sounded alongside the *Mackenzie* and found less than two feet of water abreast of the starboard deckroom

*Grounded barges
at Rosedale,
Mississippi, sitting
high and dry
three days after
we grounded on
a fast-falling
river.*

door. I knew we were in trouble. The pilot had not stopped
the paddlewheel and with every turn of the wheel more sand
washed under the boat. We knocked loose the wires that connected the boat to the barges. Then, somehow, by hook or
by crook and the help of the good Lord, we were finally able
to get the *Mackenzie* free of the sand and floating.

The river was falling so fast that we were lucky to get the boat
off of the sandbar. Forty-eight hours after we grounded, we were
able to walk around the barges, and the deckhands picked up the
rigging that had fallen in the river when we grounded and the tow
broke up. I tried to call the office on the boat's radio and give
them the "good" news, but was unable to get through. About daybreak I took the *Mackenzie* across the river and landed at Terreen Landing, where I found a large number of gasoline-filled oil
drums. Thieves had stolen gasoline from some barges that were
tied to the bank while their boat double-tripped. I walked into
the town of Rosedale, a mile or two away, to find a telephone. I
found one at the general store—probably the only phone in town.
By nine a.m., when I got back to the landing, the thieves had
hauled off all the gasoline drums. They were so quiet that nobody
on my boat even heard them.

CHAPTER 10

• • •

The company sent us to Memphis to pick up a dredge belonging to the La Crosse Dredging Company that had been dredging in the mouth of the Wolf River. Mr. A. M. Thompson owned the dredging company and was president of the Central Barge Company.

While the *Mackenzie* was tied up at the Memphis levee waiting for the dredge to gather up its equipment, we lost our cook to drowning. He had gone to town after dinner and got drunk. When he was returning to the boat sometime after midnight, he evidently missed the ladder that led from the riverbank up to the fuel flat and fell into the river face down. I discovered him the next morning when I went down the ladder to go to a telephone. One of his feet was out of the water and hung on the levee. He was a nice man and a good cook. I hated to lose him, but he let the old demon rum get to him.

We took the dredge to Terreen Landing. When we arrived where our barges were aground near the mouth of the White River, I had to go over to the hotel in Rosedale to get Captain Vier and his wife. There were no living quarters on the dredge. It was hot weather, and the hotel had no air conditioning. Who did at this time and place? The rooms all had screen doors and big louvers in the doors for air circulation—there really was not much privacy for the guests. It took about three weeks to pump the oil cargo from the grounded barges into barges that were in deep water and then dredge the barges off. After the oil was pumped out of each barge, the dredge pumped the sand out from under it and it would slip into deep water. Altogether we were there for thirty days. The dredge carried a crew of twenty-one, and with our crew we were feeding and boarding forty-five people. My

⚓

THE PERILS OF DOUBLE-TRIPPING

At the top of the bank at Terreen Landing, I walked past twenty-five or thirty oil drums filled with gasoline. Someone had been stealing gasoline from barges tied off by a boat while that was double-tripping. This was a common practice during World War II because gasoline rationing was so strict. When a boat was double-tripping, its barges might be tied off for a day or two, giving thieves plenty of time to steal gasoline. Whenever I had to tie off barges to double-trip and had to leave a watchman, I always told the watchman that if anyone came and wanted the oil, to just go to other end of the barges and let them have what they wanted. We were not bothered too much because we were towing crude oil and it would not burn in cars. I never had fuel stolen from my barges, but it was a bad experience for the boats that did.

A boat tied off some gasoline barges at Ashport, Tennessee, while double-tripping, and when it came back to pick the barges up, there were two dead men on one of the barges. The barges were loaded with casen-head gasoline, which is very volatile. The two men were asphyxiated by the gas fumes when they raised a hatch on one of the tanks and started dipping out the gasoline with a bucket. This barge had raised hatch openings and the men were doubled over into the hatch opening, where the fumes asphyxiated them

wife joined us at Memphis and worked in the galley since we had such a big crew to feed.

While we were at the mouth of the White River the crew picked up three puppies from a wild dog on the bank at White River and were taming them on the boat. A few days before we were going to leave, I told the crew to put them back on the bank, as we would be departing upriver. A cou-

Transferring cargo from grounded barges at Rosedale.

ple of days after we left, the first mate came and told me the dogs were still on the boat and he couldn't find them. So he and I went back and hunted through every room—with no luck. We found out later that the crew had ganged up and moved the dogs from room to room while we were searching for them. Each room had both an inside and outside door so it was not difficult to move the pups. Who do you think was carrying the food to the dogs from the galley? My wife! She had a big laugh over it after we put the dogs off at the Memphis levee a few days later.

• • •

The first evening after we left Terreen Landing northbound, I found the wife of the dredge captain wedging a chair under the doorknob in the room where their ten-year-old daughter would be sleeping. I told Mrs.Vier she didn't have to worry, because none of the crew would bother the child. She said, "Oh, captain, I'm not worried about that, but Jane walks in her sleep." She was sleeping in an after room on the Texas deck and there was no outside handrail around the after half of the Texas deck. I posted a man outside of Jane's room every night until we got to Memphis. I was

The Mackenzie
leaves Rosedale
after freeing the
grounded barges.
PHOTO BY AUTHOR

relieved when we delivered the dredge to Memphis and the Viers got off.

• • •

The White River incident was the only serious grounding the *Alexander Mackenzie* had on the Lower Mississippi River while I was on the boat. She did have a bad grounding at Buck Island the year before I joined the boat, but I don't believe they had to lighter the barges to get them off

After getting off the ground at Rosedale, we went on to North Bend, Ohio, and unloaded, then back to Marrero, Louisiana, for another trip. Northbound at the mouth of the White River we ran right over the spot where we'd been aground a month before. That's what happens with the river going up and down and the reason a pilot has to be well posted at all times. Our pilots were well posted, but we were unlucky enough to get caught in a shutout fog before the days of radar.

• • •

The *Mackenzie* had a grounding at Sliding Towhead above Cairo, Illinois, in 1940. I was on the *W. A. Shepard* and we tried to assist in getting them off, but were unable to free

The Mackenzie
*aground at
Sliding towhead
above Cairo,
Illinois.*

them. They had to have the Corps of Engineers dredge *Ste. Genevieve* pull the barges off. The dredge spudded down above the grounded barges and used its heavy swing cables to pull the barges off the bar. If they kept a steady pull on the cables, the current would wash the sand away, allowing the barge to move towards the dredge. It was slow work, but the dredge pulled all the barges free.

⚓

MORE INCIDENTS

On one trip, I was northbound early in the evening around Burr Oak and first mate Clay Hanlin was in the pilothouse with me. We were discussing his love life. He was dating a very lovely girl, and they were planning to get married. All of a sudden, we realized that I was running the wrong side of the red buoys. Luckily I got stopped before any real damage was done. I think we did break a wire or two.

• • •

On another trip I was pilot on the W. A. Shepard. *I walked into the pilothouse about ten o'clock in the morning. We were*

Continued on next page

headed up along Sterling Island and Captain L. J. Sullivan was laid well back in his chair with his feet cocked up on the indicator reading a magazine. I said, "Hey, Sully, aren't you on the wrong side of those red buoys?" Did he ever get busy in a hurry! He had run behind about six or seven buoys. Luckily there was enough extra water that he hadn't grounded.

• • •

A captain who was on the W.S. Rhea told me he was southbound at Lifers Light with fifteen loads and the river was up and running. Suddenly he woke up to the fact that he was sliding down behind a red buoy on the end of a rock wing dam. It was too late to stop, so he steered hard to starboard and by the grace of God had enough water to go over the dike and get back into the channel. It scared the daylights out of him. The man was a very good pilot.

• • •

We were southbound out of St.Louis with the L. Wade Childress *and twenty-five loaded barges. The* Lillian Clark *was down ahead of us and had engine trouble, so she backed in at Flora Creek to make repairs. My pilot was at Devils Field, ready to cross over to Flora Creek, when the* Clark *completed the repairs. Her pilot, instead of waiting until we were clear, backed out in front of us. The tows did not hit, but the maneuvering put us out on the bar, and we grounded and our tow broke up. Ten of our barges went on down the river behind the* Lillian Clark. *Luckily there was a Federal Barge Line boat northbound above the Cape Girardeau bridge. He was able to corral our barges and get them back to us before they slammed into the bridge. Later, the* Clark *hit the bank at Sliding towhead. We went around her and arrived in Cairo ahead of her.*

• • •

I had my first class pilot's license from Helena, Arkansas, to Cincinnati, Ohio, at this time. I ran roof-master below Memphis and stood a pilot's watch above there, but being roof-

master was a full-time job. Some of the deckhands were only fourteen or fifteen years old and some mates were pretty green. Once I went down on deck and looked around and asked Red to run second mate. Second mates did not have to be licensed. He had only been on the boat for five weeks and it was the first boat he'd ever worked on. He said he couldn't handle the job. I told him to give it a try and I would work with him. I will say he turned into a very good man.

• • •

The Alexander Mackenzie *had to quadruple-trip a place called Yellow Bend. The river was so swift the boat could only push two barges at a time. The Corps of Engineers clocked the current in the bend at fourteen miles per hour. I was not on this trip; Captain Dusty Rhoads was running master. He went up to the pilothouse at 6:00 a.m. and the pilot had the lead barge shoved halfway underwater. The water was all the way back to the middle of the barge—why it didn't dive I don't know. Dusty stopped him. The barge was almost sunk; it had been taking water through the vent holes and if Dusty hadn't come up to the pilothouse when he did, they would have lost the barge. Water was lapping over the deck of the barge, so the crew rigged some barge pumps. When they opened the hatch cover to drop the pump hoses into the bilge they had to quickly stuff blankets around the hoses to seal off the opening into the bilge. That was too close for comfort. They were able to get the barge pumped out and did not lose it.*

11 The M/V Monrola and Other Tales

In 1944, the Central Barge Company purchased a boat called the M/V *Monrola*, a single-screw, diesel boat, around 800 horsepower. I was only on her a day or two. The *Alexander Mackenzie* had her in tow from someplace on the Lower Mississippi River to Cairo, Illinois. There were only an engineer and striker on board. The *Mackenzie* was unable to push her whole tow through Yellow Bend, and since there were several other tough spots upriver, they decided to tie off half her tow and double-trip to Helena, a distance of 140 miles. They tied some of the barges and the *Monrola* to some trees on the left bank with two lines. Chief Engineer John Lynch and the striker (an engine room worker who oils and does cleanup work) on the *Monrola* were left to fend for themselves and to watch the barges.

The *Mackenzie* was gone for five days, but after only a day, the bank where the Monrola and barges were tied started to cut away. Each day the chief engineer and striker had to move the lines farther inland to new trees so they wouldn't break away. This meant moving one head line farther into the trees, easing the barges down into that line, then moving the other line farther into the trees, and then evening up the strain on the two lines. It was a taxing job for two men, and they were probably scared to death that the barges and the *Monrola* would get away from them, stranding them on the bank. I'm not sure they could have walked through the bottom to the main shore had they become stranded. I returned from vacation and caught the *Mackenzie* at Helena. The chief engineer on the *Monrola* was my brother-in-law, and was he ever upset with me! Although I was not on the boat when they tied off, he still blamed me for the situation.

• • •

One night we were southbound with eight empties and a fuel flat on the *Alexander Mackenzie*. About 3:00 a.m. the pilot hit the bank in a fog. The first mate woke me and told me the head spiked barge was missing. No broken wires—the barge was just gone and the wires were hanging over the head of the barge it had been wired to. I couldn't believe what he was telling me, so I had to go out and see for myself.

	BARGE	BARGE	BARGE	
SPIKED BARGE	BARGE	BARGE	BARGE	TOW BOAT
	BARGE	BARGE	BARGE	

Diagram of a tow with a spiked barge on the head. This is the way our tow was made up when the pilot hit the bank head on.

Around 8:00 a.m. the fog cleared. We were below a little point and had to shove up the river to see the spot of impact. When we came around the point, there was the barge stuck up on the bank at about a forty-five-degree angle! You could probably have driven a load of hay under the barge and not have knocked any hay off. We put a line on the barge and pulled it off. Placing it back in tow, we proceeded down the river.

• • •

On another trip, the same pilot hit the bank in a fog and knocked off two empty oil barges and a fuel barge. We backed into shore and waited until the fog cleared. I then dropped the *Mackenzie* down the river. A mile below us was a DPC towboat pushed in against the bank. I knew the chief engineer, Harry Bounds. As we eased by, he came out on the deck and hollered that we had a couple of barges floating in an eddy just below them. We found the two empties, but no fuel flat. We figured that it had sunk, because when the barges had swept past the *Mackenzie*'s fire room door, the fireman could see that one of the empties was on top of the end of the fuel flat.

I decided to go on down the river and keep looking and hoping. I had just about given up hope and was getting ready to call the office to tell them we were way down on the Lower Mississippi with no coal on the boat and no fuel flat when we came around a point, and lo and behold, there was a very pretty sight. The fuel flat was sitting aground on the head of a sandbar. We were able to work on into the barge and get a line onto it, pulled it off the sandbar, put it back in tow, and went on to Marrero, Louisiana. What a relief for me!

• • •

One pretty day we were coming up the Lower Mississippi River when a slender willow tree decided to visit the engine room via the starboard engine room door. It was three or four inches in diameter and about twenty-five feet long. It came through the door, up to the overhead, then wove itself through the various water and steam pipes located there. It went halfway across the engine room. Amazingly, it didn't rupture a pipe. We must have had a guardian angel, because no one was nearby and no one got hurt. The engineers cut out as much of the tree as they could, but a good part was so tightly woven into the pipes that they never could get it all out and just painted it white like the rest of the engine room. It was still there when the boat was laid up for good.

• • •

I've had several experiences over the years with snags raising barges out of the water or breaking barges loose in the tow. On one trip on the Lower Mississippi we were northbound and taking fuel out of our fuel barge. In order to reach the coal we had to drop the barge back about sixty feet or

OIL BARGE	OIL BARGE	OIL BARGE	OIL BARGE	OIL BARGE	TOW BOAT
	OIL BARGE	OIL BARGE	OIL BARGE		FUEL BARGE

Normal tow makeup on the Lower Mississippi River with the fuel flat dropped back so the towboat can take fuel.

so. A snag went under our tow and came up just at the right angle to catch the fuel barge and tear it loose. Luckily, the stern lines stayed intact, so we didn't have to chase the barge down the river. The deck crew just pulled it back to where it belonged and continued coaling.

We had a so-called "safety man" in the office at this time. He called and told me that if I had made up the tow properly, the incident wouldn't have happened. He and I didn't get along very well—I didn't believe he knew anything about towboating—and he didn't—and I told him off and set him straight. He wasn't around very long.

• • •

The *Alexander Mackenzie* was pushing up the Ohio River at a place called Chenault Reach. About 3:00 a.m., something awoke me and I heard the mate holler to the pilot, "She's all right, go ahead." I jumped out of bed, ran to the door and asked the mate what had happened. He said, "Oh, we just lost a couple of bucket boards." I hollered for the pilot to stop the paddlewheel and went back to the stern to take a look. We had lost two complete buckets and wheel arms across the whole width of the paddlewheel.

I told the pilot to get into the bank as soon as he could and not to work the boat any harder than necessary. If we had gone ahead we would have stripped the whole paddlewheel in a short time. We landed on the Ohio shore and tied off. I called Bill Trierwieler, head of maintenance, and he drove down from Cincinnati. Although we carried some replacement arms and bucket boards, we didn't have enough. First, Bill had to find a sawmill. Then they had to locate a white oak tree from which they could cut a twenty-five-foot log. Then they had to cut the tree down, saw it into lumber the size we needed, and transport it to us so that we could rebuild the wheel. Our wheel was twenty-five feet square, so it took a good-size tree to give us enough lumber for the wheel arms and buckets. I doubt if you could find a white oak tree that size today. We spent three days repairing the wheel.

Eventually, the company built a new wheel. It was made of steel out to the circle, with stub wheel arms beyond the circle to bolt the bucket boards to. I supervised the installation of the new wheel at the Corps of Engineers dry dock at Louisville. It took three days to complete the job. The new paddlewheel took much less time to maintain than the old one did.

• • •

During the coal strike in the spring of 1940, I was sent to the *Sylvia T* as pilot, and we made a trip to Chattanooga, Tennessee, on the Tennessee River. This was before the Kentucky Dam was completed. When the dam was finished, several small towns were inundated with about fifty or sixty feet of water. Our tow consisted of barges of shelled corn. While we were going through one of the locks, a girl standing on the observation platform hollered to the mate, "Mister, what have you got in them thar barges?" He hollered back, "Corn." She then asked, "On the cob or whiskey?" She had never heard of shelled corn.

• • •

In the early 1950s I was on "Old Rags" (M/V *New Orleans*) southbound out of St. Louis with sixteen loads. Two Coast Guard officers were riding to Cairo with us because their buoy boat was in the St. Louis shipyard for maintenance. (A buoy boat is a Coast Guard vessel that sounds the depth of the water and places marker buoys in the channel to indicate good water.) One officer was the captain, who had been on the buoy boat for a couple of years and was being relieved by the other officer, who just wanted to see the river he would be working on.

At this time, there were spots between St. Louis and Cairo like Calico Island, Hat Island, Platin Rock, and Devil's Backbone where you had to be on your toes because of bad turns, shallow water and the like. I was steering down in the Calico Island country and the Coast Guard officer asked me how I liked his channel report. (The Coast Guard put out sailing directions and a buoy report every week.) I didn't want to insult him, so I gave him the latest report and told him to read the directions off to me and I would try to steer by them. We had barely started when he said, "You can't steer these marks—no way possible." He tore up the report and said to me, "Have I been putting this junk out for two years?" I told him, "I'm afraid you have."

He then started to write a new report. He said that no one had ever told him his reports didn't work for towboats. The buoy boat, with a small barge ahead of it, had no trouble filling his marks, so he thought he was doing a great job, but it was impossible for a towboat and tow to do it. This is why it's good for buoy boat captains—and also lockmasters and lockmen—to travel as guests on a towboat once in a while. It lets them learn and gather the information pilots need around locks and gives them ideas for improvements in navigation aids.

• • •

I was on the *Sylvia T* with a captain whom I shall not name. We grounded at Mulhern Field on the Upper Mississippi River about 8:00 a.m. We worked all morning trying to get the tow off the ground and I could see we were going to be there several more hours. We had orders to call the office anytime we were aground more than an hour. About noon I asked the captain if he had called the office. He said, "No, if they want to know where we are they can come and find us." When I went off watch and to bed at 6:00 p.m. the tow was still aground. About 9:00 or 9:30 p.m. a deckhand woke me and said I was needed in the pilothouse. I got out of bed, dressed and went to the pilothouse. There stood our marine superintendent, Captain Connie Ingersoll, Jr. He had driven to Clarksville, Missouri, and hired a fisherman to take him downriver to where we were so he could get aboard. He greeted me, then said, "Watch her. The captain and I want to have a little talk." They left the pilothouse. After the little chat that captain never again failed to call the office if we ran aground or had a long delay.

• • •

Salvage rig raising a sunken barge above Dam No. 22.

Sunken barge just breaking water at Dam No. 22.

While I was on the *Rita Barta*, we were helping the Valley Line Salvage Rig raise a sunken barge at Lock No. 22. A Federal Barge Line boat had grounded some distance above the lock and while they were getting off the ground a barge got away from them. A cement barge had broken away from a dock several miles upriver, and the river was high and swift at the time. The current carried the barge into the dam, where it sank on top of another barge loaded with cement, which was already sunk against the dam.

It was an interesting experience. The salvage rig would pull the barge up a little above the bottom and we'd tow the whole thing into shallower water, then repeat the operation. They did get the barge up, but it was so badly damaged they had to tear it apart and take it out in pieces. The cement and scrap were used to help build up a short wing dam above the lock.

12 Ice and Wintertime Operations

For two winters, 1950 and 1951, the United States Coast Guard chartered the M/V *Central,* M/V *A. M. Thompson,* and M/V *Peoria* for icebreaking service on the Illinois River. I was captain on the *Central,* Gene Wood was captain on the *Thompson* and Mark Lancaster was captain on the *Peoria.* The *Peoria* was a new 3200-horsepower diesel boat the company had purchased in the spring of 1950. We helped various commercial tows to keep moving and regulated traffic through the ice gorges. The worse ice gorges on the Illinois River would usually form at Bull Island above Ottawa, Illinois, and at Chillicothe, Illinois, at the head of Peoria Lake. I had some interesting and exciting times working in the ice.

The first year working for the Coast Guard we started out in Joliet, Illinois. The Coast Guard had a unit called the Amsterdam Plow. Similar plows had been used in the canals of Holland, but they were not much good on our Western rivers. The Coast Guard commander in charge of icebreaking was in Joliet to see us get started. He told me to pick up the Amsterdam plow, which was tied off at the Brandon piers. He said, "I know you don't want it, but pick it up and get it out of town. Stick it behind an island—somewhere out of sight. Go ahead and do your job and when you're finished, pick the plow up and bring it back into town." And that's what we did. The Amsterdam plow stayed behind an island below Morris, Illinois, until we brought it back at the end of the ice season.

• • •

We were helping the boats in the ice above Lock No. 26 near Alton, Illinois. Captain Gene Woods was on the *A. M. Thompson* and I was on the *Central*. I was abreast of Meyers Point when I saw that the ice was moving—piling up and going over the point. I called Gene and told him to take a gander at Meyers Point and told him I was getting out of there and heading for the lock. Gene took one look, and since he was headed upstream, he said he was going to get out of there, too. We both well knew what ice can do when it gets moving. You're helpless no matter what horsepower your boat has. About half a mile or so above the *A. M. Thompson* was a boat headed south. The captain called Gene and asked him for help to the lock. Gene said, "I'll help you by shoving you back out of here, but no way am I going the other way with this ice breaking up." That is what they did.

That night I had the *Central* pushing into the No. 26 lock wall just above the lock gates to keep the ice from jamming down on the gates. About 10:00 p.m. the lockmaster called and asked me to walk out on the dam with him. We walked about a third of the way across the dam and stopped and watched the ice. There were big fields of ice—maybe four or five acres in size—coming down and hitting the piers of the dam. They jarred the dam so hard that the handrails rattled. After a few minutes, I said, "Red, I'm getting off of this dam."

He agreed with me that we'd better get off. One wonders how the dam took the punishment of being hit by those huge pieces of ice weighing thousands of tons. No wonder it shook. (This was the old Lock & Dam No. 26, which has since been replaced by the Melvin Price Locks & Dam.)

• • •

One day we were working the Bull Island gorge and a tow-boat was northbound with a three-piece petroleum tow. It consisted of a bow and stern unit with a box unit in the middle. When coupled together it's like one big barge, but it takes some doing to couple the pieces together in the ice once you break them apart. The broken ice gets between the barges and has to be pushed out so they can come together. We knew we could not get the tow through the gorge without breaking the couplings between the barges, which the captain refused to do. I told him we'd help a couple of boats through that were behind him, then work on his boat, because I knew we could get the other boats right through, speeding up the traffic and keeping things moving. The captain wasn't happy with our decision, but that's what we did.

We were working with the second boat when we heard the first boat check for traffic at Kickapoo Bend above Marseilles Lock. The captain on the petroleum boat also heard the call and immediately called his boss in Houston, Texas. He told him a big lie—that we refused to help him. (This was before the days of cellular phones, and we overheard his radio conversation.) It wasn't 15 minutes later that the commander of the Coast Guard in St. Louis, our immediate boss, called and asked what we were doing. I told him and he told me to stop whatever we were doing and start assisting the petroleum barge.

I called the captain and asked him what he wanted us to do. He tried to put the monkey on my back, but I told him to tell us what he want us to do, because evidently he was running the show. He told me to face up to his tow of three barges with the other three boats waiting to get through the gorge faced up behind me. He would get out ahead of his barges with a towing line. He was sure we could make it through the gorge, because we had about three-quarters of a mile of open water to make a lot of headway. We obeyed his request, knowing what would happen, and *it did!* As soon as he hit the ice, his boat started to go sideways ahead of the barges, but the boats on the pushing end were all backing and were able to get the tow stopped before they rolled him over and under his barges. No doubt he had to change his drawers once everything was stopped.

The captain then called and wanted the Coast Guard officer aboard the *Central* to come over to his boat. When the officer got there he could tell the captain was shook up. The captain said he realized that we could have rolled his boat over and he had been a fool. He wanted to apologize to all of us for his stupidity, and he would do what ever we wanted in order to get his tow through the gorge. He had his deckhands remove the coupling wires the barges were lashed together with and replace them with loose ropes so the barges could bend around the tight turns in the gorge, and in no time we had him through. We helped him couple his unit back together by washing the ice from between the barges. He was going up the river in a very short time, a much wiser captain.

The next summer I saw the Coast Guard commander in St. Louis and he told me what had happened that Sunday. The owner of the petroleum boat received the call from the captain. He immediately called his congressman from Texas, who immediately called the commandant of the United States Coast Guard in Washington, D.C., who called the commander in St. Louis who was our boss, who called me. This all happened on a Sunday afternoon within about fifteen or twenty minutes. Politics!

• • •

During the winter of 1948. I was downbound with the *A. H. Truax,* one empty barge on the head of the boat and seven empties on a line behind the boat, working through the ice gorge at Chillicothe. We were halfway through the gorge when it decided to let go, and away we went with the ice— nothing we could do but be eyewitnesses. We ended up with the *Truax* shoved out on the bank in front of Chillicothe, high and dry. Our starboard propeller was completely out of the water and the port propeller was halfway out. It took three other boats working in unison to jerk us back into the river.

• • •

I've seen other boats in the same predicament. The M/V *George T. Horton* got shoved out on the bank at Bull Island when a gorge broke. We were just eyewitnesses, not helpers. When an ice gorge breaks, it may have a head of water from three to seven or eight feet built up. The water has a lot of power, and it will take whatever is in its way.

• • •

One winter we were on our last trip of the season for the Upper Mississippi. Usually we carried one boat back north, deadheading it. This year we had orders to pick up nine empty barges, northbound, which I thought was foolish. We took them to St. Paul along with the *W. S. Rhea,* a dead boat. (A dead boat is a boat without a crew and not running its engines

M/V A. H. Truax *and M/V* Glen Traer *and a third boat mule training in heavy ice above Henry, Illinois.*   PHOTO BY AUTHOR

being towed by another towboat.) We picked up twelve loads of grain and started south in a very heavy snowstorm. By the time we got to Lock No. 3, there was about twelve inches of snow on the ground and it was still snowing. With this kind of a snowfall and a low temperature, the river starts to ice over very fast. We were already breaking ice above Lock No. 3. It was a Sunday afternoon, but I thought I should call Captain L. J. Sullivan, the marine superintendent, at home and tell him we were going to be in serious trouble and would need help. I knew the company had the *A. D. Haynes* laid up at St. Louis for an emergency. After I talked to Sully, we departed the lock and went down the river. When I got to Point-No-Point in Lake Pepin about 10:00 p.m., the ice was so heavy that I was having trouble steering. Then coupling wires started breaking, and to make matters worse, we were pulling timberheads out of the barges, which made it difficult to wire the barges together. We kept working and managed to keep moving.

The next morning I found out that Sully had called Captain Clay Hanlin at home and told him to get to St. Louis as quickly as possible and try to get the *A. D. Haynes* underway northbound by midnight to come to our aid. We finally got the tow to La Crosse, but we had stripped so many timberheads off some of the barges that we had to leave nine barges in an ice harbor up the Black River for the winter. They had to repair the timberheads the next spring before the barges could be towed. The *W. S. Rhea* had left St.Paul with six barges and caught up with us. The *A. D. Haynes* arrived on the scene, her head covered with several feet of ice, almost to the top of the towing knees. The three boats working together finally, after a struggle, got the nine barges to St. Louis.

• • •

Another year I was on the *L. Wade Childress,* working along with the *W. S. Rhea* and *A. D. Haynes.* We had four loads of grain and had just got ahead of a 10,500-horsepower boat that had a dead boat alongside. Another boat was helping with that boat's tow. We were all working in a gorge, but not too successfully, when the fog closed in. We were rigged with the *W. S. Rhea* and *L. Wade Childress* abreast of each other, pushing on the four barges, with the *A. D. Haynes* faced up on the bow with her stern downriver. We'd push the *A. D. Haynes* down into the ice and he'd come ahead, washing us a hole in the heavy ice. It worked very well. We'd been doing it every since Keithsburg, Illinois. The fog shut us out abreast of Crider Island, above Clarksville Chute.

After several hours the fog hadn't cleared, but Captain Hanlin said he could see enough on radar, so we could move.

M/V A. D. Haynes II.   PHOTO BY AUTHOR

We were concerned that the ice gorge would break and get us all in more trouble. We started and were able to get through just as the whole gorge turned loose. We were lucky to be out of it. We went on downriver and made Lock No. 24 at Clarksville, Missouri. The other boats, including the 10,500-horsepower one, were carried downriver below Crider Island. Luckily, they didn't end up aground, since there was enough water under the island to float them.

Unless you've been in an ice gorge and seen the ice move, it's hard to imagine the power ice can exert. I've seen big concrete navigation light piers slowly pushed over as if a big bulldozer was shoving them. After a gorge breaks, it cuts out a channel, and when you go through it, you'll see ice walls on either side, almost like concrete walls. During the winter and in ice conditions on the Illinois River, we used an oper-

Red Rock Landing after an ice gorge had broken.

ation we called "mule training." Whenever the ice got so thick that we couldn't push the tow and steer it, we'd put one barge on the head of the boat to help her handle, and string out the rest of the barges in a single file behind the boat on loose lines—maybe four or five feet between them— and away we'd go. This worked fine as long as we had enough ice to keep the barges from whipping and in a straight line but . . .

On one trip I came out of Havana, Illinois, on the *Central* with one loaded barge on the head of the boat and seven loaded barges behind the boat on lines. I was really trucking up the river until I came to Turkey Island and the ice thinned out. I didn't slow down in time and looked back to see the barges breaking lines and going everywhere; a couple of them tried to climb the bank. The crew and I managed to get them all together and pushed them the rest of the way to Peoria lock. Above the lock we had to string them out again and "mule train" them to above Spring Valley.

• • •

During the fifties and sixties, no matter where I was working, the company always transferred me to the last boat of the season coming out of St. Paul, Minnesota. One year I was on the *Central* southbound with twelve loads of grain. We had been doing fairly well until we were below Lock No. 15 at Rock Island, Illinois, at Horse Island below the I-280 highway bridge. The channel from the lock to Horse Island had been clear except for a lot of shore ice. We tried to make the turn at Horse Island, but the ice was too heavy. While I was backing and filling, trying to make the turn, the shore ice above us broke loose and followed us down, packing in around and behind us. Soon we were in an impossible situation.

I told Herb Beaver, the second mate, to break the couplings between the barges so we could railroad them out of the bend. He went out and broke them apart, but made the mistake of standing on the wrong barge when he knocked the last wire off. The barges immediately moved apart and he was stranded. It took some doing, but eventually we got the tow strung out and proceeded down river to Lock No. 16. At the lock, I was told to call our office. It seems that when I said on the morning schedule that we were working in the ice, some of the powers-that-be in the office really got shook up. I called the office, and marine superintendent Captain Sullivan, who had been out of town, walked into the office just as I called and answered the telephone. He wanted to know what was taking place, and I told him just a normal wintertime operation, nothing unusual. He said he might come up. I told him to come on— we had a belly full of fuel and lots of groceries—but he did not show up. Some office personnel who were not river people were really shook up about the ice, but we had it every year and knew how to cope with it and keep the tows moving.

Mule training in ice on the Illinois River.

That morning at Lock No. 16, I asked the lockmaster if we could change the locking procedure. I wanted to lock the boat and one barge through first, then pull the other barges into the lock behind us. It would take several lockings but would save us the job of putting the barges all back together, just to string them out again below the lock. He said it had never been done before, but he was willing to give it a try. It worked fine and saved all of us a lot of extra work.

⚓

LIFE ON THE ALEXANDER MACKENZIE

The Alexander Mackenzie *was a coal-fired, sternwheel tow-boat that carried 360 pounds of steam pressure when she came out in 1938. The steam pressure was later raised to 390 pounds. Originally, she was rated at 1,600 horsepower, but after raising the steam pressure they rated her at 1,800. She was one of the last three sternwheel steam towboats to be built. The Str.* Jack Rathbone *and Str.* Jason *were the other two.*

During World War II, the Defense Plant Corporation built twenty-one twin-screw, 2,000-horsepower steam towboats. The DPC towboats were originally supposed to be diesel, but because so many naval craft were being built, diesel engines were in short supply, so the decision was made to put steam engines in them.

The Alexander Mackenzie *originally carried a crew of twenty-five. We use to make our own potable water for drinking and cooking, as well as our own ice. We bought milk in ten-gallon cans and beef and pork a side at a time—the cooks cut it on the boat. We had ice cream twice a week, on Wednesdays and Sundays. The deckhands cranked the ice cream freezer, a job they didn't mind. The striker engineer*

• • •

Once we had a new lady boat dispatcher who was taking the morning traffic. The captain on one boat reported his position and then added that he was "mule training." The dispatcher said to someone in the office, "I didn't know the Valley Line had any mules." We teased her for a long time about it.

• • •

In the spring of 1943, I was captain on the *W. A. Shepard,* 1350 horsepower, towing coal from Havana to Joliet on the Illinois

*pulled ice, in hundred-pound cakes, every day. The deck
crew coaled the boat every day from a fuel barge or fuel flat
barge we carried alongside. The coal was transferred to the
boat by a boom and clamshell rig. The* Mackenzie *was very
luxurious inside. There was deep wool carpeting in many
areas, and where there wasn't carpeting, there was heavy
battleship linoleum. There were large rooms for the crew. Her
original cost was $360,000.*

The Mackenzie's *one drawback was that she was a coal
burner (stoker fired) and burned thirty-five to fifty tons of coal
every twenty-four hours and threw out tons of cinders. We used
standard barges—175 feet by 26 feet—as fuel flats, and every
morning the deck crew set up the the fuel flat and booms for
coaling. Once the booms were set up, one crewman loaded the
coal while the rest of the crew swept down the whole boat,
which would be covered by five or six inches of very black cinders from the previous day's burning. They dumped the cinders into the river through a canvas chute. This was done
except when we were in a lock or landing—then the cinders
were disposed of later. But the crew wasn't idle at locks and
landings—if they had spare time they'd tighten bolts in the
paddlewheel, which was twenty-five feet in diameter and
twenty-five feet across.*

River. We had picked up eight loads of coal at Havana and were
upbound. We'd had lots of rain and the river was rising very
rapidly. About11:00 a.m. the United States Corps of Engineers'
ChrisCraft speedboat from the Peoria District came down the
river and pulled alongside the *Shepard*. The boat operator came
to the pilothouse and told me to call my office immediately,
and if I couldn't get through on the radio, he was to take me
to a telephone. Naturally, I could not get through on the radio,
so he took me to Kingston Mines, Illinois, and I located a

Ice walls after an ice gorge had broken, Middle Mississippi River.

telephone. Captain L. J. Sullivan, our marine superintendent, told me to tie off my tow at a safe place and proceed light boat to Peoria as quickly as possible. The Corps of Engineers would give me instructions when I got there. They did.

The Corps had a digger boat taking sand out of the river and putting it on flat-deck barges. We would push the barges into the levee, where as soon as the barge stopped, two gangways were put down. A steady stream of men and women would then come on, fill the sandbags and carry them off. They were sandbagging the levee, trying to save the Caterpillar Plant from a fast rising river. During the first twenty-four hours they had 24,000 people working on the levee, and then they broke up into two shifts, 16,000 in the daytime and 8,000 during the night. This operation went on for three days, and they did save the levee. It was a well organized setup, with toilets and lunch wagons available so the workers did not have to take any time off, just keep filling and placing the sandbags. A public address system that you could hear a mile away was mounted on the High Bridge so those in charge could contact anyone they needed in a hurry. There were no portable radios or phones available at this time. The old levee was not high enough to keep the water back, willows had been allowed to grow up on the outside, and no doubt groundhogs had burrowed a lot of holes in the levee. When I was pushing the barge into the levee, I had to have fairly good headway to get through the willows, but not be going fast enough to touch the levee. It was a very nervous and stressful time for me, because both the head of the Peoria District of the Corps of Engineers and the Caterpillar Plant manager were standing right behind me in the pilothouse saying things like, "Don't knock a hole in the levee—it will be at least nine months before we can get the plant back into operation." This was during World War II, and the Caterpillar Plant was a major production location for the war effort.

• • •

In the late fifties, I was captain on the Str. *Tennessee*, and Captain Robert Richtman was the pilot. We were southbound with fifteen loads on the Upper Mississippi at Cuivre Island, mile 235.0. Bob grounded around 4:00 or 5:00 a.m. Our loads were all drawing nine feet, but the Tennessee was drawing nine feet plus and there was only nine feet in the crossing. The tow went over the reef, but the boat did not. It was Sunday morning and the island right below where we grounded was lined with yachts and houseboats, all tied up for the week-end. We tried all day to get over the reef with the boat. We dropped the tow down a little from the boat, holding it with two manila lines. Finally, just about dark, the lines parted and the tow got away. It raked down the island, where all the boaters had been tied up. Luckily, by the grace of God, just before the lines parted the last boater had left. Shortly, we were able to get the boat over the reef and we caught the tow before it got into any more trouble. We then went on down the river. What we didn't know was the M/V *Double D* had been aground at that spot all day Saturday. She had kicked up a lot of lumps trying to get off the ground. She finally got off and went on up the river, and the crew didn't say a word to anyone about having been aground. Today you cannot do that, as all groundings have to be reported to the Coast Guard as soon as they happen. Also, lock personnel know if a boat has been unduly delayed between locks and will ask questions.

While all this was happening, the majority of the small boaters were smart and stayed well clear of us and our wheel wash, which was really swirling because of the very shallow water. But one fellow kept getting too close and was in danger of getting into serious trouble. We found out that he was a well-known river pilot from the Missouri River who should have known better! I guess he was trying to show off in front of his friends.

• • •

Trying to work a sternwheel boat in the ice on the Illinois River in the wintertime was rugged. Six- to ten-inch ice was very hard on a wooden wheel, and one winter the crew had to rebuild the wheel three times. The company even tried putting sheet iron envelopes over the bucket boards to protect them from ice damage, but that wasn't successful. It made the wheel too heavy and the envelopes wouldn't stay on the bucket boards

• • •

In 1940, when I was pilot on the *Alexander McKenzie*, we received orders to take some barges from Cairo, Illinois, to Paducah, Kentucky, on the Ohio River and return. Since neither the captain nor I were licensed on the Ohio River, we picked up a trip-pilot at Cairo, Illinois, Captain John Trail. We went on to Paducah that afternoon. I was in the pilothouse as we approached Lock No. 53, with Captain Trail doing the work. Carl Hall was chief engineer, and he always kept the boat hot—we had a full head of steam. The boat carried 360 pounds of steam pressure, and the smokestacks were on either side of the pilothouse toward the back.

As we approached the lock, Captain Trail rang for a slow bell. I knew what to expect: just before the boilers popped off there would be a slight hissing sound for a split second before the loud explosion when the boilers' safety valves popped off—first on one side and then on the other. I thought Captain Trail was going to leave the pilothouse when the first side popped off! He turned and saw me just sitting there when the other side let go. He told me I should have warned him since this was the first steamboat he'd been on since the Str. *Clyde,* which had blown up while he was on watch at Grand Tower Chute in 1937. He had gone out through the pilothouse roof and was severely injured. Luckily, the port smokestack didn't come down at the same time and place that Captain Trail did. After that experience, it's a wonder that he hadn't had a heart attack when the *Mackenzie* popped off, for it sounded like two cannons being fired.

• • •

We had made up twenty-five loaded barges and four empty barges with the *Valley Transporter* at St. Louis to go to Cairo, Illinois. At the last minute the office called and told us to add one more empty, a tank barge. We had orders to never put a tank barge on the head of the tow, but to place them back in the tow so they were covered up and protected. But we were ready to depart, so I said to the mate, "Heck, there's nothing to hit between here and Cairo—just stick it in the notch on the port corner on the head." Famous last words . . .

Remains of the Str. Clyde *after she blew up in Grand Tower Chute, 1937.*
COURTESY MURPHY LIBRARY, UNIVERSITY OF WISCONSIN - LA CROSSE

The crew stuck the barge in the notch and we departed for Cairo. About 2:00 a.m. the pilot was steering down around Brunkhorst and Fountain Bluff. The first mate, who was in the pilothouse with the pilot, said, "Skipper, your stern is getting awfully close to the bank." He said, "Oh, it will be all right." He hardly had the words out of his mouth before CRASH! The stern of the *Valley Transporter* hit the bank and knocked the boat out of tow. Everything let go except one wing wire. The crash woke me, and I jumped out of bed and ran to the pilothouse. As I ran up the stairs I could hear the pilot cussing a blue streak. When I showed up, he said the other boat had run him out of the river. Well, the "other boat" was a small boat with one or two barges and it was way over on the Missouri shore, so I could see that it hadn't run him out of the river. I took over the controls. The first mate and his deck crew were on the ball and managed to get several

Valley Transporter
with tow.

parts of line between the *Transporter*'s cathead bitts and the tow so I could start backing and try to flank down around Fountain Bluff. There was a fairly strong current down the bend and we were floating very fast. The whole shore was lined with huge boulders and one after another they went out of sight under the empty tank barge on the port corner. I was expecting it to hit at any moment. Somehow we missed all of the rocks and finally got back out in straight river, where we rewired the boat back into the tow. Then we proceeded down the river with a big sigh of relief.

• • •

During World War II the government took an LST that had seen action in the South Pacific and outfitted it as a museum and display of war memorabilia. It was touring the Mississippi River system, stopping at towns and cities on a war bond selling mission. One foggy morning I was northbound on the *Alexander Mackenzie* on the Ohio River, just below French

Island. I suddenly realized there was a vessel broadside to the channel and immediately ahead of me. I immediately started backing and throwing the head of my tow away from him. It was the war bond LST, which was painted in South Seas camouflage and nearly impossible to see in the fog. He had been at anchor all night and was getting ready to get underway southbound. It was halfway turned around when I spotted it. Luckily we missed each other. It was a scary situation, to say the least. It would have made big headlines if we had collided.

• • •

We had another entanglement with an LST, northbound on the Ohio River with our regular petroleum tow above Lock & Dam No. 53 in open river conditions with fog. The pilot could see a white light above the fog, so was holding on it, thinking it was the white light atop the water tower at Joppa, Illinois. Neither the Joppa power plant nor the cement plant had been built at this time and the water tower light was the only light visible at night. About 3:00 a.m. the pilot was suddenly aware of a bell striking. He tried to kill out his headway, but didn't get it stopped before he zeroed in on an LST that was anchored in the middle of the river with both a bow and a stern anchor out. Our lead barge ran right up the stern anchor cable and hit the stern of the LST dead center. It did not damage the LST but put a dent about four feet deep into the center of one of our petroleum barges at the head log, just the shape of the LST's stern.

The Coast Guard investigating officers were not very happy, especially since we did not have a lookout on the head of the tow. The officers boarded us at Lock No. 52 and questioned me first. I told them I was in bed asleep and was quickly informed that that was no excuse. Mike Moll, the first mate, who was on watch, had asked the pilot if he wanted a lookout and the pilot had said that it wasn't necessary. After that, anytime a dark cloud went over the moon, Mike Moll didn't have to ask the pilot if he wanted a lookout, because there was already a man on the head of the tow. The mate never did tell me what the Coast Guard officers said to him, but whatever it was, they made a believer out of him.

• • •

Another story about the *Mackenzie* and an LST: I was home on vacation when it happened, but came back in time to get involved in all the paperwork. The *Mackenzie* was northbound at night out of Marrero, Louisiana, with a loaded oil tow. She was meeting an LST, and the LST was coming almost straight at her. Suddenly the pilot steered for a port-to-port meeting, but was too close. She hit the outside head corner of the port lead barge, cutting about eight or ten feet off the corner of the barge like it had been sliced with a knife. The LST was sliced open for 161 feet starting just aft of the hinge of the bow door. The first eighty feet was opened about two feet wide, the rest just a few inches. Some of the oil in the barge slopped into the LST, starting a fire. A fire also started on the barge, but Carl Hall, the chief engineer of the *Mackenzie* ran out with a blanket and smothered it before it could get really started. Some crew members on the LST were overcome by smoke, but all recovered. The damage was about two feet above the water line, so the vessel did not sink. The LST was loaded for departure overseas. It had small ammunition aboard, plus a full complement of Marines. The only thing they were lacking was their heavy ammunition, and they were en route to pick that up. Part of the damage went right though those heavy ammunition compartments. Luckily, the heavy ammunition was not aboard or there would have been a real catastrophe.

We were using battery running lights at the time. The batteries were of very poor quality and we had to replace them about every six hours. The pilot on the LST thought the *Mackenzie* was running light boat. He didn't see the running lights on our barges until too late to avoid a collision.

13 Various Stories

In 1940 the *Shepard* was southbound on the Ohio River, near Brown's Island. The wind was blowing very hard straight up the river, making big waves that were breaking over the head of the tow. We had to back in and wait for the wind to die down and the waves to subside. The engineers had an old washtub they used to wash engine oil filters in. The striker had been setting the tub outside on the deck, always in the way. On this day, it was on the port side deck when a big wave came over the side and washed it away. The striker came running to the pilothouse and wanted permission to put the yawl in the water and retrieve his tub. I told him, "No way—it's too rough for the yawl." So it was good-bye washtub. I wasn't sorry to see it go.

• • •

In April of 1941, the *W. A. Shepard* was sent to Cincinnati, Ohio, on the Ohio River. Going up the river, the chief engineer's stepson, who was a striker on the *Shepard* and lived in New Amsterdam, Indiana, came to me about 7:00 a.m. and asked to get off at Cedar Branch Light so he could go home for a few hours and then catch the boat at Louisville. The Cedar

Branch navigation light was on the Kentucky shore. The boy said he knew the way across the point and he'd have to walk only a mile or two through the woods and across the hills to be abreast of his house in Indiana. It was eighteen miles to New Amsterdam by river around a long bend in a very beautiful section of the Ohio River known as the Ox-bows.

The boy said he could get someone to row him across the river to New Amsterdam, so I landed and let him get off. It was a cold, rainy April day. He became lost in the woods and hills but finally made it across to the other side. Six hours later, we were coming up below New Amsterdam and saw a yawl being pulled across the river just ahead of us. With my binoculars, I could see the striker in the yawl. When we got to Lock No. 41 at Louisville, Kentucky, that evening, he got aboard and we heard his story. Before he left the *Shepard* that morning, he had borrowed (without asking) the chief engineer's brand new dress shoes to wear, and when he reached his home the shoes were soaked. He placed them near a potbellied heating stove to dry out and in the process he ruined them. Needless to say, the chief was very upset. I don't know if he made the boy buy him a new pair of shoes.

• • •

We were locking up at Lock No. 8 on the Ohio River. The deck crew had just pulled the first locking out and tied it off on the upper guide wall when around the corner above the lock came an outboard motorboat, running wide open down the middle of the river. There was a small creek bar a short distance above the end of the lock wall and the two characters in the motorboat turned into this bar, never slowing down until they were beached out of the water, high and dry. We departed the lock and went up to Lock No. 7, where the lockmen asked us if we had seen the two motorboaters. They had come down above Lock No. 7 out in the middle of the river. There was about six inches of water running over the top of the dam and they made no attempt to slow down. They flew over the top of the dam and pancaked into the water below, a drop of about eight feet. When the lockmen saw them coming, they knew what was going to happen. One of the lockmen jumped into the rescue boat and rowed out to where they had landed. One of them hollered over to the lockman, "Hey, how do you get around these d——— things anyway?" Makes you wonder why there are not more serious accidents on the river than there are.

• • •

I was northbound on the Upper Mississippi with the *W. A. Shepard*. She had eight barges of coal in tow. We had tied the tow off in the trees across from Red Wing, Minnesota, to deliver one barge into the slip there. The river was very high and the riverbank was completely under water, leaving only the trees we were tied to sticking out. After delivering the load, we pushed up the river to Lock No. 3. Because of a breakdown of the lock gate machinery, we had to wait for a couple of hours. About 6 p.m., after the repairs were completed, we proceeded up the river. I was on watch and kept smelling a skunk. I said to the chief engineer, "Boy, there are sure a lot of skunks in this neck of the woods." The deckhands were busy carrying unused barge rigging back off the tow and they made numerous trips. I don't know why they didn't discover the skunk. At Lock No. 2 we used the small chamber (the big chamber had not been built yet) and had to do a maneuver we called a jack-knife with the barges. In order to fit into the lock chamber, some barges were moved so the tow was three wide instead of two wide. After locking, about 3:00 a.m., the crew finished putting the tow back together and the *Shepard* proceeded up the river. The first mate was coming down between the barges, now rigged two wide. He threw his leg around a timberhead (a fitting on the deck to tie lines to) and felt something move. It was a skunk! He ran but was not fast enough—the skunk sprayed him but good. The worst part of the story is that at midnight, when he had come on watch, he had put on all brand new clothes, including shoes. He threw the whole caboodle into the river. No wonder I was smelling skunk all the way up the river that evening!

• • •

You get all kinds of crew members from all over the country on a towboat. One deckhand—I'll call him John—was allergic to soap and water. I got on him one day about bathing and he said he had run out of his special soap. I said, "John, you knew when you left home how long you were going to work, so you should have brought enough to last you. That's no excuse." A day or so later he claimed to be sick and got off the boat. A few weeks later I came back from a vacation and he was back on the boat, but the next day he again claimed he was sick and got off. He told the office he wanted to transfer to another boat, which he did. Guess what? The next time I came back from vacation I was sent to *that* boat. As soon as John saw me come aboard, up to the pilothouse he came, and said he was sick and had to get off. I don't know where he finally ended up, but wherever it was, he probably needed a bath.

• • •

While on the subject of bathing, here's another good story. During World War II, we hired a fireman from Lawrenceburg,

Indiana, on the *Alexander Mackenzie*. He had been working on a digger-boat there unloading coal barges for a coal company incline. He had been on the boat several days and evidently was not bathing. One evening I was walking back to the crew's mess, and just before I entered I overheard the crew talking, so I stopped and listened a few moments. Their talk went like this: "We ought to give him [the fireman] a bath." "No, the captain would pay us off." "I don't think he would."

I then walked through the mess room and said, as I walked by, "Hi boys, the G. I. brushes and laundry soap are in the laundry room underneath the sink." I kept right on walking down the passageway.

One deckhand said, "Did you hear what the captain said?" Another spoke up: "I know what he meant—let's go!" They gathered up the G. I. brushes and the strong yellow laundry soap. Some others dragged the poor fireman out of his bunk. I was told later the man hadn't been that clean or that pink since the day he was born. All the rest of the trip, during supper someone would say, "Tom, have you had your shower yet?" He wouldn't even finish eating his meal, but would jump up and run for the shower—but he did stay clean. He stayed on the boat for a month or two.

• • •

While the *W. A. Shepard* was at Minneapolis waiting for loads, the striker and his buddy went to town, forgetting to come back until almost watch time. It was August, and hotter than Hades. The chief engineer said, "Well, he has to learn," so he put him to sooging (scrubbing) the overhead fidley in the engine room, and that cured the striker of staying out all night.

Then we had an engineer who wore shoes with soles that picked up oil and swelled until finally they were like boats; the edges were at least an inch high all the way around. Some of the crew hid the shoes one day and the poor guy was in pain for days trying to wear a regular pair of shoes.

• • •

One August afternoon, about the time the Beatles and long hair were popular, I tied off on the upper lock wall at Lock No. 9 waiting for my turn to lock. There was an Alter boat locking down ahead of me. I went out to use the telephone and as I was coming back to the boat, the lockman stopped me to have a chat. He was laughing about an incident he had just witnessed. He had pulled the first locking of the Alter boat out of the lock chamber and was walking back to get the second part of the tow. A young deckhand with very short hair fell in beside him. The lockman asked the deckhand where his buddy was. The boy said that he was ahead of them. The lockman said, "No, the one with the long blond hair." The deckhand said, "That was me. I couldn't stand that d—— wig another minute." The lockman didn't believe him, so he turned around and walked back to the lower gate and looked down on the tow. There on the deck lay the deckhand's blond wig. Can you imagine anyone decking with a wig on in ninety-degree weather?

• • •

During the winter months in late 1930s and early '40s, the United States Corps of Engineers, along with the United States Lighthouse Service and later the United States Coast Guard, would remove all the buoys and float lights from the river by November 15 and not replace them until the middle or end of March to avoid ice damage and loss. The buoys were lighter and had smaller anchors than the ones in use today. We ran anyway, buoys or no buoys. We still had the lights and day boards on the banks to assist us. During periods of high water on the Lower Mississippi River if the light stand was flooded out, the light tender would simply hang a kerosene lantern in a tree. Surprisingly, we had very little difficulty. This did make good pilots, though. We really had to learn the river. You'd be surprised at some of the places that you could run when the buoys were missing, the water a little high or the ice thick and tough—like behind the light at Detweiller Park Light. Today most of the backwaters have filled in because during very high water a lot of mud and sand is carried into the river from erosion of farmers' fields.

• • •

Before the early 1940s, the navigation lights were all run on oil or kerosene. The light tenders, frequently commercial fishermen, usually had a number of lights to take care of and got paid so much per light, which gave them a little regular income. Then the battery light was developed, and today some navigation lights are connected to power lines or are solar powered.

• • •

The *Glen Traer* had two women working in the galley—sisters-in-law we called the Gold Dust twins for reasons I don't know. One was the cook and other the maid. The chief engineer, Ralph Crocker, was always playing some kind of trick on them. One day when he got up he placed a very real-looking plastic spider in his bed under the covers. The maid, Beulah, went to make his bed, threw back the covers and there was this big spider. She grabbed a pillow case and captured the thing and ran down to the galley to show her sister-in-law, scared to death. Everyone had a big laugh.

• • •

The *Glen Traer* was southbound above the Marseilles Canal, which led down to the Marseilles lock. The water was high, so there was a lot of current and a boat was double-tripping up around Kickapoo Bend below Seneca. They'd tied some of their barges to the wall leading into the Marseilles Canal. One end of the barges had broken loose and floated out crosswise, blocking the entrance. The *Glen Traer* came around the corner and the current was so strong she was unable to hold up above the canal. The pilot tried to squeeze by the barges and into the canal but didn't make it. The *Glen Traer* went out on the dam and sank. No one was hurt in the accident. The chief engineer told me he was working in the lower engine room when the boat went into the dam. He had to pull himself up the steps with the water pouring down on top of him. It's a good thing he was a big, powerful man. Later the boat was raised and ran again. After that accident the Corps of Engineers made a rule that no one could tie off barges at the head of the canal and they cut the mooring cavels off so there was nothing to tie to.

• • •

On one of our trips on the *Alexander Mackenzie,* we shoved out of the Marseilles Canal not knowing the river was rising very fast, and the lock personnel at Dresden Island Lock & Dam were opening up more dams above us. We got up to Kickapoo Bend and stalled out. We had no choice but to back down out of there, because we could not get to the bank. The channel is cut through solid rock and there is no way to get to shore. After dropping down out of the rock cut a little we were able to shove into the right descending bank across from Blanchard Island,

M/V Glen Traer *sunk against the Marseilles Dam.*   PHOTO BY AUTHOR

beneath a small creek bar that gave us some protection from the current. There wasn't anything to tie to and I knew we wouldn't be able to make it back into the canal. There was a towboat in the canal, but he was afraid to come out into the very swift current to help us, and I did not blame him. We ended up having a shore crew come from the Joliet maintenance shop and dig a place to put three "dead men" in a farmer's corn field. To make a dead man, first you dig a hole five or six feet deep. Then you fasten wire around a couple of railroad ties and bury them with the wire sticking out so you can tie to it and stay safe even if you lose power. We stayed there until a day or so later when the current slacked off, and the whole time we were working the boat full ahead!

• • •

One bright and sunny morning I was southbound on the Ohio River on the *Louisiana* just below Lock No. 46, coming down around Owensboro bar. There was not much water over the bar and there was a couple in a small boat on the high part of the bar. My tow pulled all the water off the bar, leaving the couple stranded. The young man, instead of just sitting there, jumped into the water and was going to push the boat back into the water. He no sooner got into the water than the water came back onto the bar, soaking him thoroughly. Live and learn!

• • •

I saw the same thing happen on the Upper Mississippi at Minneiska, Minnesota. Half a dozen men in a large houseboat were trying to cross the sandbar abreast of Minneiska at the same time the *W. S. Rhea* was coming down the bend with fifteen loads. The *Rhea* sucked all the water off the bar and the men were trying to shake the boat loose to get it to move, but they were actually headed out into shallower water. All they had to do was wait a few minutes!

• • •

I left Lock No. 6 at Trempealeau, Wisconsin, northbound with fifteen loads on the *Rita Barta*. She was 6500 horsepower and threw a considerable wheel wash. I looked back and I saw a young couple in a motorboat cutting back and forth through the waves from the wheel wash. I could tell the girl was scared to death, but the boy kept getting closer and closer to the stern of our boat. Then he hit a big wave and the boat dived into it, but did not come back up until it was completely filled with water. (It was built with flotation foam in it, so it did not sink.) The last I saw of them they were floating down

the river and paddling the submerged boat to the shore—
probably the end of a beautiful friendship.

• • •

I was northbound on the Illinois River on the *A. M. Thompson* with fifteen loads, running behind the *Neville,* which had
fifteen barges in tow consisting of a string of loads down the
middle and empties on either side. Two men in an outboard
motorboat tried to run through the first coupling from the head
of tow while the *Neville* was moving up the river. They made
the first thirty-five feet, the width of a barge, then they hit a
loaded barge and were rolled under the tow. The deck crew
could hear them hollering at the couplings on their way back,
but they never came out from under the tow and could not
be saved. About a week before this happened the two men
had been in a tavern in Pekin, Illinois, arguing about whether
this very thing could be done. They had been fishing—and
probably drinking—all day. They found out that it could not
be done, but it cost them their lives. We had to hold up behind
the *Neville* for several hours until their bodies were recovered.

• • •

It was the last trip of the season. We were northbound at the
Lower Winona railroad bridge about 5:00 p.m. with the *Rita
Barta* and twelve empty barges to load out with grain in the
Twin Cities. As we approaching the bridge, a very heavy
snow squall hit us. I was in the pilothouse with the pilot, Captain Dickie Pope, and two deckhands were on the head of
the tow, one on either corner. This bridge had 200 feet horizontal clearance and our tow was 105 feet wide. Captain
Pope got the tow into the bridge draw without any difficulty, but at the same time the deckhands on the head of the
tow and we in the pilothouse could hear, on the tow speak-

er, a motorboat crossing just ahead of us. The lookouts could not see the boat because of the snow, and all of a sudden the sound of the motor quit. We didn't know if we had run over the motorboat or not. The snow let up a little so we pushed up to the Winona powerhouse dock and landed. I went to a shore telephone and called the sheriff and Captain Sullivan, our marine superintendent in St. Louis. The sheriff and a couple of deputies came to the powerhouse and we were discussing what to do when one of the deputies asked, "I wonder if Tom Jones could have been out in his boat?" He was noted for poaching and very well known to the Sheriff's Department. The sheriff sent the deputy down to talk to Tom Jones. He denied having been out in his boat, but after the deputy convinced him they were not concerned about his poaching, but wanted to get our towboat on up the river, he admitted he had been out in his boat and came across in front of the barges, shut his motor off and drifted in behind the bridge sheer fence, where he kept his boat. When the deputy came back and told us what had happened, we all were very relieved and proceeded up the river.

• • •

I was coming out of Lock No. 20 one night on the *Wheelock Whitney* just about watch changing time. A snag came out from under the tow and up through the port face wires, bending the snag back like a bow. Captain Gene Wood was on the port boiler deck en route to the pilothouse. He saw the snag and quickly got behind the corner of the deck house just as the snag bent back and finally snapped. We had a new generator set sitting on the main deck, port guard, waiting to be installed, and a three-inch pump hose was lying on top of it. The limb hit the hose so hard that it flattened like a pancake and we were unable to use it again, but it did not break anything on the generator.

• • •

One beautiful evening I was northbound on the *A. H. Truax* just below Bear Creek at Hannibal, Missouri, pushing ten barge loads of coal rigged five barges long and two wide.

I was sitting back with my feet cocked up on the console, just taking it easy. Suddenly, for no apparent reason the head of the boat started going down. I unwound myself from the console and just about had my feet on the deck when the boat gave a lurch and settled back down. I called Dean Borgeson, the chief engineer, and asked him what had happened, but he didn't know. He had been sitting on the port bull rail outside the engine room door, enjoying the evening. He was looking forward and saw the head of the boat suddenly going down and the stern lifting up out of the water. I had stopped the engines by this time so they wouldn't run away. After the boat settled down, we continued on up the river.

M/V A. H. Truax. PHOTO BY AUTHOR

The *Truax* was scheduled to be dry-docked when we returned to St. Louis. At the shipyard, when she was lifted out of the water, Borgeson and I carefully checked the hull. The only thing we found was some paint rubbed off on the port Kort nozzle's leading edge. Evidently a snag had caught the Kort nozzle at just the right place to act like a pole vault and jacked the stern up out of the water before it slipped off. Luckily there was no damage.

• • •

I was on the *Alexander Mackenzie*, northbound on the Ohio River during high water. I had crossed from the Indiana shore to the Henderson, Kentucky, riverfront to pick up an electrician. I had slowed down to make a yawl play when the port lead barge bow suddenly rose up out of the water about two feet or so, then quickly dropped back down. There was a huge tree floating down the river with the butt end sticking out of the water just enough to catch the head log of the port lead barge and jack it up like a pole vault. Luckily for us, there was no damage to the barge or tow.

• • •

There is stretch of river on the Upper Mississippi that is fairly straight, with several islands scattered on either side. This stretch, which looks just like the actual channel, snakes between the islands and the Iowa shoreline. At that time, the channel went from Spechts Ferry to Rosebrook Island, passing the Finley day mark. Hurricane Island came next, then on to Cameron light and up the Iowa shore. It is normal procedure for a pilot going off watch to tell his location to the man coming on watch so the new man knows where the boat is, especially when it is pitch black outside. At midnight on one very dark night, the captain and pilot were changing watches on the Str. *Patrick J. Hurley*. The captain told the pilot they were just passing Rosebrook Island. The pilot disagreed and told the captain they were at Hurricane Island, and after arguing for a few minutes the captain shrugged his shoulders and left the pilothouse. Very shortly the mate showed up in the pilothouse, where the pilot was laughing. The pilot asked the mate if the captain sent him up. The captain had; he had told the mate, "That pilot is lost and doesn't know where he is—go up and keep an eye on him." The pilot was laughing because he had known all along that they were just passing Rosebrook Island—he was just enjoying a joke and trying to shake the captain up.

• • •

There was a captain on the *Patrick J. Hurley* who liked his coffee *hot,* and every night at nine o'clock he wanted a cup of coffee. Evidently the galley horse wasn't doing it quite right, so the captain told him he wanted his coffee at nine o'clock sharp, not one minute before or one minute after, but at nine o'clock, and he wanted it *hot.* Right after supper the next night the galley horse put an empty coffee cup in the oven, which was heated with fuel oil, and was always on and hot. Just before 9:00 p.m., he went to the pilothouse with a very hot cup of coffee, stood outside until nine o'clock sharp, went in and said, "Captain, here is your coffee and it is *hot."* The captain took the cup and saucer, touched it to his lips and told the galley horse it was fine, just right. It was so hot he had to let it cool before he could even take a sip. No more complaints about hot coffee.

• • •

The *Patrick J. Hurley* had several heavy steel doors on the boiler deck in front of the boilers. These were usually open and held up with hooks to let the heat from the boiler room escape. One night the crew got together and decided to play a trick on the pilot. The boat was going downstream and would be running a close bridge (a bridge without much horizontal clearance). In fact, they usually landed on the sheer fence trying to get through this bridge. (A sheer fence is a wooden structure constructed of piling driven into the riverbed and faced with heavy timbers. It directs a vessel into the bridge opening and protects the bridge piers.) The mate assigned a deckhand to hold up each of the steel doors, ready to release them. Then he arranged the rest of the practical joke with the engineer: at the moment of impact, when the tow was landing on the sheer fence, the engineer would pull the main electrical switch, shutting off all the lights, including the searchlights. At the same time, the deckhands would let all the doors bang down at the same time with an enormous crash. The plan worked: They did land on the sheer fence, the lights went out, and the boiler doors clanged shut. The poor pilot just about had a heart attack. Fortunately, there was no damage, just one shook-up pilot.

• • •

On the Ohio River in the 1930s there was a small steam towboat, about 350 horsepower, called the *Plymouth*. She was southbound with a tow of barges and her pilot was a very nervous type. Every time he reached a tight place, he'd get a call from mother nature. He always got the urge when he was at a spot where it was impossible for him to leave the pilothouse. The first mate said he was going to break him of the habit. The mate knew that about 3:00 a.m they would be coming to a very close place called Highland Rocks where you had to flank the bend close to the point because the

Highland Rocks came well out into the river on the bend side. Lock No. 49 was just below the Rocks, and with open river it was necessary to run the pass in the dam. The mate took a bucket, cut the bottom out of it, and gave it to the galley horse. Right on schedule there was a toot on the whistle and the pilot asked the galley horse for a bucket. Once mother nature had been taken care of, the galley horse removed the bucket. It was a dark night and the pilot was a pacer. All night he walked from one side of the pilothouse to the other. You can imagine what the pilothouse looked like by morning. That pilot never asked for a bucket again.

• • •

I was on the *L. J. Sullivan* during the summer of 1978, north-bound between Winnebago and Campbell's Island. The weather report was thunderstorms, some possibly severe.

Two friends were riding with me from Lock No. 15 to Lock No. 14. They and the chief engineer, Billy Price, were on the deck outside the pilothouse when the chief called me to come out and look at the clouds overhead. I had never seen anything like it. The clouds were swirling in a circular motion and on the inside rim lightning was flashing as if a giant emery wheel was turning. Within minutes we saw the tail of a tornado come down. The electrical wires at a trailer park we were abreast of were sparking, and we knew there must be damage in the park. The tail then crossed about 800 feet to the stern of the boat, picking up water like a water spout. It was raining so hard that I was lucky to keep the tow in the channel.

A towboat locking down at Lock No. 14 turned a search-light downriver to aid me so I had a light to head on and could stay out of trouble making the crossing to the lock. We found out when we arrived at the lock that a big houseboat had tried to land on the upper lockwall and the waves created by the storm had sunk it along the upper guide wall. We had to wait at the lock until a salvage outfit came, raised the boat and moved it clear of the lock.

• • •

The year hurricane Gilbert came ashore on the Gulf coast it traveled up the Mississippi Valley as a tropical storm. I was on the *Mississippi Queen* coming up below Lock No. 15 and I'd had high winds all afternoon. Captain John Davitt came on watch at Lock No. 15, and the wind was blowing at sixty miles per hour when he departed the lock. As he was crossing from Campbells Island to Lock No. 14, an Alter boat was locking southbound and ready to depart the lock. If the Alter boat had waited at the lock until the *Mississippi Queen* had crossed to the Iowa shore, everything would have been fine— the *Queen* would have been in the shelter of the bank and trees. But he didn't wait. When Captain John had to stop to let the Alter boat clear with a sixty-mile wind blowing straight across the river, the *Queen* was blown out of the channel into the rocks. No damage except we sat there all night until about noon. The wind then slacked off and we were able to get off the ground and underway with the assistance of two of Shorty Williams's tugs.

14 *Changes*

The Upper Mississippi River between Cairo, Illinois, and St. Louis used to have what we called "hurdles," which were wing dams constructed of wooden piling driven into the riverbed through mats made of willow trees woven together and weighted down with rock. The piling were then tied with wire and woven together with cross piling. The hurdles did a fair job of helping to control the channel, but some were washed out in high water and the winter ice was hard on them. The Corps of Engineers also tried using concrete piling instead of wooden ones but that didn't work at all. Then they started putting in rock wing dams, and those have done an excellent job. Also, the Corps has used thousands of tons of rock to riprap the banks to help control erosion. In some places on the Lower Mississippi, the Corps has graded banks and laid concrete mats—like paving—to control erosion. When I was running the Lower Mississippi in the 1940s, there were no rock wing dams and very few wooden hurdles. The channel shifted much more then than it does today because of the control measures the Corps of Engineers uses.

It's interesting to see the changes in places where I used to run boats—like Craighead Point, Trotters above Helena, Arkansas, and Six Mile Island at Hickman, Kentucky. In some places where there was no land, an island has built up with big trees growing; in other places there was an island but it has completely washed away. Once in 1945, I landed with my whole tow at the city front at Hickman to put a man off to go to the doctor. Now the city front is about a mile from the channel and has large trees growing in front of it. You have to go up a canal to get to the city front.

The Upper Mississippi has had several major changes since I first went up it in 1939. There was a place called Hole-in-the-Wall where the channel went between two islands; the channel ran between the islands and down the Illinois shore past the mouth of the Galena River. On down a bit it crossed back to the Iowa shore. Today we go straight down the Iowa shore past Gordon's Ferry. At Smith Bay there used to be a very tight couple of turns to get around an island. The Corps of Engineers dredged the channel behind the island several years ago, and now you just go down around the back side of the island—much easier and better.

We use to run by Dallas City, Illinois; now we go the point-way and stay completely away from Dallas City. Lock No. 19 had a small lock—110 feet wide by 360 feet long—with a floating wooden sheer fence both above and below the lock. It was necessary to break up the tow and lock three barges at a time. The crew and lockmen really got a workout locking, but I'll say one thing: the lockmen at Keokuk, Iowa, were always more than willing to help put the tow back together. They used their haulage winch to pull the barges together so the deck crew could wire them in place. In 1957 the small

Prairie du Chien pontoon railroad bridge, showing one of the three ice-breaking piers above the bridge. PHOTO BY AUTHOR

lock chamber was replaced with a 1200-foot by 110-foot-wide chamber. The new lock has floating mooring pins, which is a big help. The lockmen don't have to pull the heavy two-inch lock lines up thirty-eight feet to tie off with. In the 1980s the Corps sealed off the small chamber, which was deteriorating and unsafe, so it could not be used.

Numerous wing dams in the St. Paul District have been cut off or shortened to give more room around the bends. There use to be pontoon railroad bridges at the foot of Lake Pepin, at Read's Landing and at Marquette, Iowa. These bridges were operated by steam-powered winches that pulled them open and closed. When Lock and Dam No. 25 was first completed, there was a large bay below the end of the lower lock wall. Today it has mostly filled in, with large trees growing where the bay used to be.

Among other changes over the years is a big lock chamber, 600 feet by 110 feet at Lock No. 2, Hastings, Minnesota. The old chamber was 500 feet long and 110 feet wide and could only lock three barges at a time. The swing span on the railroad bridge at Hastings was replaced with a lift span.

The old span made many a pilot sweat—it was close and very treacherous. A new highway bridge was built at Hastings, too, replacing the old spiral bridge that had been built to handle horse and buggy traffic before the days of automobiles. Many more new highway bridges have been built: at Red Wing, Minnesota; Prairie du Chien, Wisconsin; two at Dubuque, Iowa; the I-80 bridge at Leclaire, Iowa; the I-74 bridge at Bettendorf, Iowa; the I-280 bridge at Davenport, Iowa; Alton, Illinois; and also a new set of locks replacing Lock No. 26, the Mel Price Locks. One chamber is 1200 feet by 110 feet and the other is 600 feet by 110 feet.

The railroad bridge at Keithsburg, Illinois, was removed. The bridge had not been in use for years when three boys climbed up to the control house one night to set off some fireworks. The sparks flew into a pile of oily rags and soon had the control house in flames. The bridge was raised at the time and the fire caused the span to collapse, shutting down river traffic until it could be cut out of the way. A deputy sheriff was cruising around that night and saw a car parked in a strange location not too far from the bridge. He jotted down the license plate number, so the boys were apprehended. Later the Corps of Engineers took out another bridge span and pier, which made a lot more room to navigate the bridge.

In the early morning hours one day in 1941, a steam locomotive was coming across the Keithsburg railroad bridge. The bridge was raised, and the locomotive was pushing a coal tender. The coal tender hit the counterweight and the tender's front wheels ran off of the bridge. The locomotive engineer climbed down from the engine, walked back across the bridge, and disappeared. I was talking to some railroad engineers in Alton about three weeks later, and no one had heard

Locomotive that tried to run off the Keithsburg railroad bridge.

from the man or knew where he was. I *do* know that someone was either asleep at the switch or not on the ball.

• • •

During low water times before the fixed dam was built at the
Chain-of-Rocks, boats had trouble getting nine-foot-draft
barges over the lower lock sill at Lock No. 26—at times there
was only seven feet of water over the lower sill. On one par-
ticular trip the company had to lighter a linseed oil barge.
Two barges were lashed together, one empty, and the oil was
pumped into the empty barge to get the heavy barge up to
a seven foot draft. Usually, when doing this, the transfer crew
ends up with one barge listing considerably, and the crew
doing this transfer did just that. We came in about 10:00 p.m.
to pick up the barges, which were not lashed or tied tightly
together. Charlie, one of my deckhands, jumped over a head-
er pipe on one of the barges and landed on a big spot of
linseed oil that hadn't been cleaned up. Away Charlie went,
skidding across the deck, not having a thing to grab hold of.

He went down between the barges about a quarter of the way from the end of the two barges. The rest of the deck crew rushed to where Charlie had gone in and threw him a line. He grabbed it and the crew started to work him to the end of the barges. I was in the pilothouse trying my best to keep the barges from slamming together. Finally, I couldn't keep them apart; they came together with a resounding crash.

I was sure that Charlie was still between the barges, but the good Lord was with us. The crew had managed to get him just clear of the rakes of the barges, so he was not hit when they came together. Once they got Charlie aboard, I was so weak that I had to sit down for a while. I was all right until it was over, but then it hit me hard. I sent Charlie to the hospital in Alton, Illinois. He was checked over and sent back to the boat none the worse for his experience, but it was very frightening for Charlie and all of us.

At Lock No. 26, the *Central* was drawing too much water to clear the lock sill. I put an empty barge on either side of the boat, pumped some water into the barges, then wired the boat to the barges. I pumped the water out of the barges and was able to lift the boat enough to clear the lock sill. A lot of work, but it got us over the sill without damaging the sill or boat.

15 An Old-Fashioned Steamboat Race

I was on the *Alexander Mackenzie* in the 1940s running to North Bend, Ohio. We were northbound on an open river at Cairo, Illinois. ("Open river" means that all the dams were down. This was when there were wicket-type dams on the Ohio River; today there are high-lift tainter-type dams.) The Str. *Talbot* and the M/V *Wm. Penn*, both belonging to the Union Barge Line, were leaving Cairo at the same time, as was the *Mackenzie*. All three boats were making about the same time, and a race started between them. The *Wm. Penn*, a diesel boat, had engine trouble in the vicinity of Owensboro, Kentucky, and had to drop out. The *Mackenzie* was neck and neck with the *Talbot* at Lock No. 41 after racing for 341 miles. The *Talbot* had the inside track, so she made the lock first, but she had to pick up a barge at Louisville and do some tow work, so the *Mackenzie* and *Talbot* departed Louisville abreast of each other.

The next morning I came on watch just below Sugar Creek, and the air in the pilothouse was blue. Captain Truman Mayfield, the pilot, was hot. He said that ———— on the *Talbot* had tried to run him out of the river several times during the

M/V William Penn, *one of the boats racing the* Mackenzie *from Cairo up the Ohio River.* PHOTO COURTESY DANIEL C. OWEN, MARYVILLE, ILLINOIS

night. The river was high enough so we were running the willows (getting as close to the willows as you can because the current is easier. Pilots call it duck water).

I said OK and took over the watch. When I got around Sugar Creek bend, I dropped into the Kentucky shore and ran the willows close. No sooner had I started, here came the *Talbot*. The pilot landed his tow on mine. Just as soon as the head of his tow touched mine he put his rudders hard down. I could see what he was doing, because the *Talbot* had a large pilot wheel and I could see it spin hard down. He was trying to push the *Mackenzie's* tow into the bank. Twice I threw him out into the river off of my tow, but he kept coming back. He just wouldn't give up. Just below Patriot, Indiana, I had to get out in the river because of the large rocks on the Kentucky shore. The *Talbot* moved a couple of hundred feet away from me. The wind was blowing from our stern and the smoke from the two coal-burning boats was blowing straight ahead of us, very thick and black. Around the bend came an L.S.T. going downriver, I blew one whistle for a port-to-port passing. The *Talbot* blew two whistles for a starboard-to-starboard passing and the L.S.T. came down between us through the smoke, probably cussing both of us. We were still neck and neck going up into Big Bone Island Chute. In the 1940s, Big Bone was a large island; it has since washed away. The Kentucky shore in this area was very rocky, and as soon as we were in the chute the *Talbot* landed alongside again. When his tow touched mine he put his rudders hard down again. He was doing his best to put me into the rocks. This was in the days of few radios, and the *Talbot* did not have one, so I was unable to talk to him. The speaking tube from the engine room whistled and Carl Hall, the chief engineer, hollered up, "If you don't beach him you're chicken." I said, "Chief, give me time, give me time." I looked out and on the *Talbot*'s boiler deck (the second deck up), chief engineer Eddie German, who knew Carl Hall, was prancing up and down with a maid's umbrella over his head, making fun of our cinders, which were blowing over onto the *Talbot*. As soon as we were out of Big Bone Island Chute and clear of Big Bone Island, I headed for the point of the Indiana shore, which was covered with willow trees. I kept pushing and just missed it by a few feet. The *Talbot* and her barges were still against my barges on the inside of me. The last I saw of the *Talbot*, the pilot was trying to get stopped and his tow was knocking down willows by the dozen. That was the end of the race. We did not see the *Talbot* anymore.

Two months later, Carl Hall was catching the *Mackenzie* at Memphis, and the *Talbot* was lying at the levee waiting for something. Carl went on the *Talbot* to talk to Eddie German.

Str. Talbot, *one of the boats racing the* Mackenzie *from* Cairo *up the Ohio River.*   PHOTO BY FREDERICK McCABE, HANNIBAL, OHIO

Eddie asked him who the captain on the Mackenzie was and called me a no-good s.o.b who ran them out of the river. He said, "We liked to never have gotten off those willows." Carl replied, "Wait a minute, Eddie. Who tried to run who out of the river?" Eddie had to admit that they had bitten off more than they could chew.

One night I made the mistake of telling this story to some of the crew on the *Delta Queen,* and a few months later ended up in the annual staged race with the Str. *Belle of Louisville* during Kentucky Derby Week at Louisville, Kentucky. I was on watch on the *Delta Queen* during the race. We were running neck and neck with the *Belle of Louisville.* Of course, all of the passengers and any of the crew who were not working were out on deck watching the race, and a number of crew members were standing in front of the pilothouse. Suddenly, some of them started chanting, "Put him in the willows, put him in the willows." Of course, none of the passengers knew what they meant. But I did.

Since then they've changed the rules for the race, and now one boat has to be on the Kentucky shore and the other on the Indiana shore—they can't be close together like we were for that race. The race officials, who live in Louisville, always give the *Belle* the Indiana side because that's where the duck water is.

• • •

On one trip the *Mackenzie* had to stop at the foot of Lake Pepin because of high wind kicking up big waves on the lake. The waves were high enough to wash over the sides of the barges and swamp them, so the *Mackenzie* had to wait until the wind died down and the waves subsided. I was on the *A. H. Truax* not too far behind, so when we arrived we tied off on the side of the *Mackenzie*'s tow. Naturally the off-watch *Truax* crew went over on the *Mackenzie* to play poker. Captain Walter Karnath on the *Mackenzie* was always bragging about how much better his boat was than the *Truax*. It was true that the *Mackenzie* was more powerful than the *Truax*, but I told him I was going to beat him into St. Paul anyhow. He said, "No way."

The wind usually calms about sundown. I had the mate post a deckhand at either end of our tow where we were tied off. When the wind died down and we could safely go, the mate ran over on the *Mackenzie* where the poker game was in progress and told our crew we were turning loose. By the time the *Mackenzie* untied their lines and pulled them in from the shore, we had a sizeable lead. We beat them across the lake and into St. Paul. Carl Hall, chief engineer on the *Mackenzie*, told Captain Karnath, "You'd better watch that Hillman, because he's going to outsmart you." It always bothered Carl when a "turpentine burner," as he called a diesel boat, beat his steamboat.

• • •

Years ago pilots use to stand what was called a "dogwatch."
It went like this: 6 a.m. to 12 p.m., 12 p.m. to 6 p.m, 6 p.m.
to 11 p.m., 11 p.m. to 3 a.m., 3 a.m. to 6 a.m. On watches
with regularly spaced intervals (square watches), one pilot
would complain that the other was getting more daylight than
he was, but with dogwatches, daylight watches shifted every
other day, and that took care of the arguing. I wouldn't work
dogwatches myself because the sleeping times were so irreg-
ular. The Union Barge Line pilots worked dogwatches until
radios came into use in the mid-1940s. Then they stopped,
because the dispatchers wanted to know who was on watch
when they called the boat; they usually wanted to talk to the
master. It did make some sense to dogwatch years ago when
packet boats were running, mostly in a short trade. They'd
depart from a town every day or so at the same time on a
set schedule. A pilot might not get over a stretch of river for
a long time if he was working a square watch and could run
into trouble if he was caught in a fog some night and wasn't
well posted over that stretch. Outside of that, dogwatches just
didn't make sense to me.

CHAPTER 15

16 *New Boats*

In April of 1946, the company built a new boat, the M/V *A. H. Truax,* a 1460-horsepower, twin-screw, Kort nozzle diesel boat. My wife and I went to Chicago for the christening party.

I became master after the boat was completed at Lockport, Illinois. Because of the low bridge clearances in the Chicago area, it was necessary to remove the *Truax*'s pilothouse and upper deck quarters and tow the boat to Lockport. At Lockport the pieces were reassembled.

When the boat was completed we came down the Illinois River to the Mississippi and ran in the coal trade between Alton, Illinois, and St. Paul, Minnesota.

We usually towed ten barge loads northbound, rigged two wide and five long.That was the only way we could shove them whenever there was very much current in the river. Southbound we usually towed fifteen empty barges.

The *Alexander Mackenzie* usually towed fourteen loaded barges plus a coal flat northbound and returned southbound with a small tow of empty barges plus a coal flat. Both the *Mackenzie* and the *Truax* worked between Alton, Illinois, and St. Paul, Minnesota, with a side trip to Cairo, Illinois, thrown in

Lifting the pilot-house, stacks, and other parts from the A.H.Truax *so the boat would clear the Chicago bridges. The* Truax *was built in Chicago by the Calumet Shipyard.*

PHOTOS BY AUTHOR

every once in a while until the end of November. We went to the Illinois River for the winter season, running between Havana and Joliet, Illinois. We always received a goodly amount of ice experience on the Illinois River during the winter months.

• • •

While I was on the *Truax* the company decided to make a test run and see if the new unit-type barges that had just been built were going to pay off. We shoved six loaded double-rake barges from Alton to Lock No. 25, then doubled back light boat and picked up six unit barges. We timed them both for the same distance. There was a considerable difference, and the company built only unit barges from then on.

• • •

When the *A. H. Truax* was built, her backing—or flanking—rudders were made too small, and the hydraulic ram that controlled them was also small. The shipyard people came down to Alton to check out our complaints and run some tests to figure out what was needed to correct the problem. We took one empty barge and ran full speed ahead doing figure eights abreast of the Alton Water Works. Our assistant engineer had been home for the day, and while waiting to reboard near the Alton Waterworks, he overheard two girls sunbathing on the bank. One girl turned to the other and said, "That's the craziest-acting boat that I ever did see." People probably did wonder about our antics, but we were able to show the engineers what was needed to correct our steering problem.

• • •

The Illinois River has seen lots of major changes since the early towboat days. In the 1930s, there was a pontoon bridge at Lacon and also one at Havana, the Old Upper Free bridge (a swing span) at the narrows in Peoria Lake, which was was hand-operated. You had to be very cautious when the wind was blowing, because sometimes the men turning the big key that opened the bridge lost control and the wind blew the bridge partway shut. One day the *Sylvia T* was northbound at the Old Upper Free bridge when the wind blew it partway closed just as the boat was getting into the bridge. Luckily, the pilot was able to get stopped inches from the bridge, but he came within two inches of tearing off his starboard searchlight, which was mounted on the corner of the pilothouse.

• • •

The old highway bridge at Beardstown, Illinois, operated the same way. At Beardstown, the bridge tender would gather a bunch of men from a nearby bar to give him a hand in very windy conditions. There were also narrow and difficult bridges at Utica, Peru, Meredosia, Florence and Depue, all of which are gone or altered today.

• • •

I was southbound on the Upper Mississippi with the *W. S. Rhea* and fifteen bargeloads of grain, when I came down to the Lansing, Iowa, highway bridge. The river there has a very sharp ninety-degree turn just above the bridge. I cut the point too close and the port string of barges started to drag very hard on the bottom near the point. I knew that if I stopped the current would carry my tow broadside into the lefthand bridge pier, so I drove the boat full ahead and she shoved off the point. The tow was going to clear the pier, but then I had to back up, because I wasn't going to make the turn without hitting the bank. I did hit the bank, and the starboard lead barge rode up on the bank and then slid down a little, but the tow didn't break even one wire. It was about 7:00 on Sunday morning and not a soul was around except a local policeman. There wasn't a thing up and down the whole shore except a single, solitary aluminum yawl, so what do you think I did? I zeroed in on that yawl and fixed it up for the scrapyard. Of course, the policeman phoned down to Lock No. 9 and the company ended up buying the owner a nice new yawl.

• • •

Coming into Pittsburgh we hadn't received any orders. On arriving the watchman at the landing gave me orders to transfer the groceries and crew to the *LTI-2194*, which was lying at the landing. She was a new experimental boat leased from the U. S. Army. Her sinusoidal propulsion units were certainly different. They consisted of a series of vertical paddles on a rotor unit. She had no rudders. The paddle unit was not only the propulsion but also the steering mechanism. Instead of having conventional Western River-type steering levers in the

—Enquirer (Bob Free) Photos

VERTICAL PROPS USED ON NEW RIVER BOAT

The first river boat in America to use vertical-axis propellers, the Army's LTI-2194, arrived in Cincinnati last week end. Housing for the vessel's two sinusoidal propeller units are under the two "pill boxes" near the stern. Two spare vertical-axis propeller blades are mounted behind them. Capt. Norman Hillman, seen handling the craft's unique steering gear, will command the LTI-2194 for the Mississippi Valley Barge Line Co. Each wheel controls one of the propeller units.

LTI 2194 pilothouse with double controls for the wheels, one for the port wheel and the other for the starboard wheel.   PHOTO BY CINCINNATI ENQUIRER pilothouse, she had two round Cadillac steering wheels, much like a car. Each wheel controlled one of the propulsion units. The wheels were of different sizes, mounted one above the other. It took some experimenting and practice to handle the boat without getting into trouble. The propulsion units did not prove to work well, and later the vessel was sold to a barge line company that replaced them with conventional propellers and rudders.

• • •

One day I was on watch on the *Alexander Mackenzie*, which was northbound on the Ohio River at Louisville, Kentucky, with ten loaded barges of crude oil and two fuel flats, in high water conditions. About halfway between the Water Works and Six Mile Island, I lost the ability to steer. I couldn't move the steering levers one way and the rudders were about halfway over. I was unable to straighten them in order to steer. I stopped the paddlewheel and the engineer started to check things out. We'd had some difficulty with the steering hydraulic valve and had replaced it with a new Luckinhiemer valve; we thought that was the trouble. Meanwhile we were floating backward—downriver—with the current. No tugs were available in the harbor at Louisville, and of course, the Louisville bridges and Dam No. 41 were there. Since the engineers couldn't locate the difficulty, I had the mate and deck crew start to jury-rig a mechanism to steer with. They got ready to disconnect the hydraulic system and ran two midship capstan lines to the tiller arms. It was time-consuming, but with the bridges getting closer by the minute, we were hurrying as fast as possible. We had the lines all laid and were just ready to disconnect the hydraulic system when the steering levers in the pilothouse suddenly became free and I could use the rudder system again. I immediately came full ahead on the paddlewheel, hoping the boat would kill the sternway before we got to the first bridge. We were less than a quarter mile above the first bridge when we finally killed our sternway and started moving up the river again. I was sweating blood. What happened was that an oiler had brought a ladder in behind the starboard boiler and leaned it against the tiller bar that went from the pilothouse to the engine room. The hydraulic valve that controlled the rudders was located in the after end of the engine room. The system had several cranks to make the turns around the various corners. The oiler had leaned the ladder against the tiller bar so that it fouled one of the cranks, blocking the movement of the tiller bars. We discovered it just in time—I'm not sure we could have gotten the jury rig going before we would have hit the bridges. We certainly would have made national headlines if that had happened!

● ● ●

Here's another steering problem story on a different boat. Captain Emil "Red" Gearing and I went north on the Upper Mississippi on the *L. Wade Childress* with orders to transfer to the *Valley Voyager* when we met her at LaGrange, Missouri. Captain Dave Holst, who was master on the *Valley Voyager,* informed us that the electric steering was out. It was kicking out at the most inopportune times, and he and his partner were afraid to trust the system. The boat had a Sperry steering system which was considered to be good. There was a small steering lever with which you could steer using just one finger, but in case of failure there were hydraulic levers to use as a backup. The hydraulic levers were very hard to move, and after a six-hour watch working them, you knew you'd earned your pay.

M/V L. Wade Childress.

Dave and his pilot had used the hydraulic system all the way from around Quincy, Illinois, to St. Paul, Minnesota, and back downriver. Every time the steering went out the pilot was on watch, and the rudders always went out at night. When Red and I transferred to the *Valley Voyager*, we didn't like tugging on those levers for six hours at a time, so we tried out the electric system. We couldn't find anything wrong with it—it worked fine for several days, until we were going up the Ohio River; then the unit went out. We quickly discovered what was wrong. On the port side of the console were two switches to switch from the Sperry system to the hydraulic system. One of us accidentally laid a flashlight down too hard and hit the switch that cut out the Sperry System. Bingo! No steering. Dave's pilot had been using a chart and

M/V Valley Voyager *and sister boats* M/V Valley Transporter *and* M/V
A. D. Haynes II *were identical. The only mistake made on the boats was
that the pilothouse was too low. The pilot couldn't see over thirty-five
barges and had to depend on radar.*

flashlight because he was not well posted on the Upper Mississippi, and apparently his flashlight was hitting the switch
when he laid it down. Dean Borgeson, our chief engineer,
cut a couple of pieces of rubber hose that just fit over the
switches. In order to push a switch you had to put your finger straight down into the hose, and that solved the problem.

• • •

Captain Jim Beaver and I were on "Old Rags," as we called
the *New Orleans,* southbound on the Ohio River. We had
almost a full double locking tow, lacking just one standard
empty barge on the starboard corner on the head. Coming
down on Lock No. 19, the river was rising very fast and there
was a lot of outdraft above the lock because some of the dam
wickets were laid down. The deck crew caught a handy line
from the lockman with no difficulty, but they had to check
the tow tight into the lock wall because of the notch on the

head where the one standard was missing. The tow had to be lined up perfectly to enter the lock chamber, otherwise it could pinch or damage a lock gate. We were doing OK except that *Old Rags* wouldn't pick her stern up, and I thought we were going to top around into the dam. I had the deck crew turn the line loose from the lock wall, backed up the river some and on a second try we made it into the lock. When we got to Lock No. 20 they were "throwing" the dam (lowering the wickets so they lie on the bottom of the river and boats can run over the top of them). We had open river conditions from there on down to Cairo except for the McAlpine Locks at Louisville.

We locked through the McAlpine lock with no problem. I shoved across the river leaving the lock to go through the Sherman Minton highway bridge. The current was stronger than I figured it to be, so I had to really push *Old Rags* to get her to clear the bridge pier. She didn't steer well, so I started her backing as soon as I was sure she would clear the bridge pier so she wouldn't hit the shore. I was trying to get her to lift her stern, which she wouldn't do. I hit the bank and slid down the Indiana shore. Because the water was so high, I hit a couple of huge oak trees standing at the top of the bank and bulldozed them over like they were saplings. Just beyond the trees was a small house that I thought the barges were going to hit, but luckily the tow stopped just in time, maybe twenty feet away. There was a car parked between the tow and the house and the owner was in the yard watching the show. All of a sudden the owner of the house said to the deckhands, who were on the head of the tow, that maybe he'd better move his car, since the barges were still sliding slowly down toward the house. He moved

M/V New Orleans, "Old Rags." PHOTO COURTESY LIBERTY MARINE, HANNIBAL, OHIO

his car, came back and said, "Maybe I'd better get my wife out of the house." Evidently, he put his car ahead of his wife. The company would have bought him a new car, but not a new wife!

• • •

On this same trip, Captain Jim Beaver got caught in a shut-out fog at Pates Hollow. He backed into the Kentucky shore and waited for the fog to lift. By the time it lifted, I was on watch. I backed out, intending to flank out and straighten up, but *Old Rags* wouldn't lift her stern one iota. We ended up going down the river sideways, the head of the tow knocking down willows by the dozen. As we passed Carter's Landing I finally got the tow around and headed downriver toward Cairo. Eventually we arrived at Cairo, delivered the tow and started back up the river with our northbound tow. I was relieved at Paducah, Kentucky, and went home for a well-earned vacation. Coming up the river the boat wasn't steering right, so the company finally decided to dry-dock the boat at the Jeffersonville Shipyard, Jeffersonville, Indiana. When she was lifted out of the water, they found the port steering rudder completely gone, the rudder shaft broken off at the hull and over half of the starboard flanking rudder missing. No wonder we couldn't pick our stern up coming down the river. It was a wonder we even made it to Cairo.

• • •

There's more—I was southbound above Cape Rock, a sharp, close place in the Mississippi River above Cape Girardeau. I decided that I couldn't make the bend without flanking, so went to backing to get in a flanking position, but there was more current than I figured. I didn't get killed out in time, and the head of the tow climbed and slid down the bank. There were two old concrete bridge piers in the way, and the head of my tow hit the upper one and very slowly pushed it over. There was no damage to the barge or tow and we didn't even break a wire. I never did hear anything about the piers, for they were abandoned. With *Old Rags* you really had to be on your toes. The only mistake the company made was not keeping her just to train young pilots. She could make good pilots cry even when she was in good shape.

• • •

Here's a little story about pushing a tow made up two barges wide and five barges long—long and narrow. Captain Sullivan, the marine vice president of operations, called me at home one day and said, "Do you know what that captain ___ on the *Truax* did? He came up below Fox Island and laid the whole tow across a wing dam and it broke up. He had broken so much rigging that we had to truck in rigging from Joliet, so he could remake his tow." I said, "Yes Sully, I know just what happened." He asked me how I knew and I told him the same thing had almost happened to me the trip before. The tow sucked up under the bar on the left bank and the stern barge hung up on the sandbar and the tow started to top around, but I was lucky and the stern barge came off the bar. I was able to get straightened up just in time. Sully didn't chew the other captain out after I told him what had happened to me.

• • •

In April of 1949, the company built a new diesel boat, the *A. M. Thompson*, 2600 horsepower. I brought this boat out of the Calumet Shipyard as a brand new vessel, was even on her the first time the engineers turned the engines over while at the dock, and was on her shakedown cruise. We ran her in the same trade as the *A. H. Truax* and *Alexander Mackenzie*, Alton to St.Paul on the Mississippi and on the Illinois River in the wintertime.

In April of 1950, the company built a third boat at the Calumet Shipyard. The *Central* was a twin of the *A. M. Thompson* except that the pilothouse was raised four feet higher, which gave the pilots much better vision. We took the boat across Lake Michigan from South Chicago to the mouth of the Chicago River with a tug towing it. The pilothouse, stacks and cabin behind the pilothouse were in a barge because of low bridge clearances between Chicago and Lockport. At Lockport they were welded into place. Unbeknownst to the welders working on the inside, the radar technicians installing the radar and radios had dumped a large pile of excelsior packing material outside on the deck. A spark from the welding caught in the excelsior and soon a huge fire was going. Luckily we were able to extinguish it without any major damage.

Gathering up barges after hitting the Vicksburg Bridge.   PHOTO BY AUTHOR

• • •

I was put on the *A. M. Thompson* in April of 1951 to take twelve barges of grain to New Orleans during a coal strike, and the coal hauling boats were laid up. My trip-pilots were Captain Davenport Day and Captain Eugene Hampton. Captain Day was on watch at the Vicksburg Highway bridge. I told him he was over-flanking the bridge and he argued with me—said he knew what he was doing. But he didn't come ahead soon enough and the current carried the tow sideways into the bridge. The result was that he sank three barges, damaged two others severely and came very close to turning the *Thompson* over. It was just by the grace of God that we didn't lose the boat. She rolled over so far that she took solid water over the bull-rail. Luckily, no one was injured and we completed the trip to New Orleans and returned uneventfully. A few years after this, a small towboat with a crew of eleven got in the same predicament and was not as lucky. It rolled over with all of the crew, and within thirty seconds all was gone.

156   CHAPTER 16

The A. M. Thompson. PHOTO BY CAPTAIN MOLL

Very tragic! My mistake was that I did not ask Captain Gene Hampton to come to the pilothouse before we got to the Vicksburg bridge. It would have prevented a bad accident.Captain Hampton was a very experienced pilot and had been on the Str. *Sprague* for years.

• • •

In July of 1952, the Central Barge Company merged with the Mississippi Valley Barge Line of St. Louis, and the merged company was called the Valley Line. Shortly after the merger I was transferred to the *Peoria* running between New Orleans, Louisiana, and Coraopolis, Pennsylvania, just out of Pittsburgh on the Ohio River. I worked as roof captain one trip above Cincinnati, then started standing a watch from Cincinnati to Pittsburgh. There were no good pilots available and I would rather stand a watch myself than have a pilot who wasn't any good—I'd have to be up with him half the time anyway.

The *Peoria* was towing a three-piece unit tow hauling alcohol. Our only complaint was when we got to Cairo northbound, the dispatchers would hang a bunch of loads on us, whatever would fit into a lock for a full double locking. Then they started doing this when we were southbound as well. On one trip they put seventeen loads on us out of Cairo besides our empty alcohol unit. We were 1100 feet long and 220 feet wide. And to make the matters worse, the *Peoria* was powered with two Fairbanks-Morse opposed-piston engines that would only back at fifty percent of their rated power. Somehow we made it to New Orleans safely, only running daylight most of the trip. If we were coming to a tough, close place we'd wait for daylight to run it.

• • •

Here's a little side story that came to me from John McMahon, who was working in the office at the time. When the dispatcher gave me the orders to pick up the seventeen loads, I called our marine superintendent, Captain A. D. Haynes, and told him we would be sadly overloaded and it was not safe. He told me they realized that, but the tow had to move and no other boat was available, so just to use my own judgment and only run daylight if I had to. So the first night below Cairo, Illinois, we stopped about 10:00 p.m. because there was a tight place to run and we needed daylight to see everything. We departed about 5:00 a.m. At schedule time I reported the fact that we had stopped. When Haynes got the message in the office, he put on a real show, hollering and cussing because we had stopped. You could hear him all over the office. This was for the benefit of the president of the company, whose office was just down the hall. McMahon told me this happened every morning until we arrived at New

Orleans. Of course, Captain Haynes was the one who had told me to tie up and wait for daylight whenever I thought we should, but such is office politics.

● ● ●

Between Baton Rouge and New Orleans we had one extremely close call. We were coming down on a fog bank, when out of the fog came a large ship, heading straight at the *Peoria*. Our pilot started to stop the engines. I was in the pilot-house with him and jumped up, pushing the throttles full ahead, and began blowing danger whistles. The ship didn't slow down or acknowledge the whistles, but it turned at the very last moment, after coming within a cat's whisker—three or four feet—of running us down. I found out later that the river pilot on the ship was not even on the bridge at the time and the wheelsman was going to hold his compass course come what may. Luckily, the pilot came back on the bridge just in time to avert a very serious accident. A short time before this a United States Coast Guard buoy tender was run into by a ship in this same vicinity. The buoy tender was rolled over and the whole crew was lost.

● ● ●

I was northbound on the Indiana just below where the new Greenup Locks are today and was due to get off in the next day or so for my vacation. At our 3:00 p.m. radio schedule the office told the pilot I was to get off as soon as possible and get home as quickly as I could. I was not to worry about relief, they would get someone to the boat. My daughter, Stephanie, was in the hospital. The pilot landed the tow against the bank and I jumped off within twenty minutes after I received the message. I climbed the steep bank to the highway, then started thumbing for a ride. Two or three cars passed me by, then a pickup truck went by. He was about a quarter mile past me when he stopped and backed up. The driver was a farmer who was on his way home after selling his tobacco crop in Maysville, Kentucky. He said, "You looked like a man who is in a hurry to get someplace." I told him my story and he took me into Greenup, Kentucky. There was no taxi in Greenup, but at a café I found a girl who was home to attend a funeral. She lived somewhere in Ohio but thought she knew how to get to the Charleston, West Virginia, airport. We got in her car, but she needed to stop at a gas station to get gas. Naturally, she met a man she'd gone to school with and had to spend fifteen minutes talking over old times. I was on pins and needles to get going. Finally we made it to Huntington, West Virginia. While we were waiting at a stop light a taxi pulled up behind us, I jumped out and asked the taxi driver if he had a fare, which he didn't, and if he knew the way to the Charleston, West Virginia, airport, which he did, so I quickly paid off the girl. I had called the Charleston airport from Greenup and explained my situation to the ticket agent. There was only one flight left out of Charleston that day. It was on Piedmont Airlines and was going to be a close connection, but I told the ticket agent I would try to make the flight if it was humanly possible.

When we arrived at the Charleston airport I jumped out of the taxi and ran into the terminal, one of the pilots was just about to go out the other door to the tarmac. The ticket agent said, "Here he comes now!" They had actually held that plane as long as they could for me. I can just see airline personnel doing that today. I made the plane connection, arrived home late that night and learned that my daughter had accidentally ingested some lye water. The next morning the doctors decided that she should be in the Riley Children's Hospital in Indianapolis. They also thought that my wife and I should drive Stephanie to the hospital in Indianapolis. We got there in record time, and when we pulled up to the emergency entrance two nurses were waiting for us. Stephanie was hospitalized for a number of days, and bringing her home a few days before Christmas was the best Christmas present my wife and I ever received.

The company and people I worked for were one in a million—they thought a person's family came first and would bend over backward to help people out anyway they could.

17 *Last Tow over Greenup Pass*

In 1959 I was on the *Indiana* southbound on the Ohio River with a full double locking loaded tow. We had nine jumbo barges and eight standard barges breasted up ahead of them. This was when the United States Corps of Engineers was constructing the new high lift locks and dams. We came down above the Greenup Locks, which were completed, but the dam was still under construction. I called the lockman on the radio and he told me I could run the pass if I wished. The construction people had two thirds of the river cofferdammed off where they were building the new dam. The area between the locks and the cofferdam, probably 600 feet, was the navigable pass. I knew the river would be really pouring down through the pass, but decided to run it.

We came down above the lock to where we could see down through the pass. Lo and behold, we could see that the Str. *Omar* of the Ohio River Company, which was not too far ahead of us, had run the pass. The only thing was, the *Omar* had run into the riverbank below the dam, and broken their tow up. I could see that the barges were out of the way, so I decided to stay with my original thinking and run

Str. Indiana *before being converted to* M/V Indiana.

the pass. What a thrill! There was a two-and-one-half- to three-foot drop and the water was really pouring through. When each set of barges went through the opening it dropped down to the lower water level. It was something to watch. I'll never know why the wires didn't pull apart and why our tow didn't break up. Captain Red Gearing and first mate Clarence Vickers were in the pilothouse with me. We figured we were making at least seventeen or eighteen miles per hour going down through the pass. The lockmen were watching us from the lockhouse, and as soon as we were in the clear, they called and told us we'd be the last tow through there—the rest would have to use the lock. It was too dangerous to run the pass with that much drop. I heartily agreed with him.

After about a year or so, I was transferred back to the *Central* running the Ohio River between Cairo, Illinois, and Pittsburgh, Pennsylvania. Every spring and fall, no matter what boat I was working on, I would be transferred to some boat on the Upper Mississippi for the first trip in and the last

M/V Indiana *after conversion to diesel power.*

trip out of St. Paul, and I received a lot of good ice experience. The first trip of the season on the Upper Mississippi was always interesting for several reasons. At night lots of people would flash their lights at us. I think it was a sign they were glad to see the boats back and running, for spring could not be far behind.

• • •

I was captain on the first boat into St. Paul, Minnesota, for eight years in a row. One trip I was on the *Rita Barta* and we were pushing six loads through Lake Pepin, breaking thirty-three inches of solid blue ice with six inches of slush ice on top of it. We stopped just below Lake City, Minnesota, and measured the ice. Of course the ice fishermen were not in love with us—we broke a path through the ice that they couldn't cross unless they had a boat.

Some fishermen were really ingenious. They put runners on the bottom of their boat, removed the propeller from an outboard motor, attached something like a saw blade that dug into the ice, and away they would go, lickety-split across the ice, and they'd usually have enough headway to carry them through any open water. They didn't worry about the small path that we opened up in the ice.

• • •

In the early 1960s, I was transferred back to running on the Upper Mississippi for the most part and was captain on the *L. Wade Childress*. The company repowered her in the mid-60s. She was originally 3600 horsepower. After repowering she had 5000 horsepower. We worked the Upper Mississippi in the summertime; then we'd go to the Ohio for the winter months, running from Cairo, Illinois, to Pittsburgh, Pennsylvania.

• • •

Another year on the first trip of the season on the Upper Mississippi, we had six loaded barges and six empty barges with the *L. Wade Childress*. We'd push the loads through the heavy ice, tie the barges off to a good tree, then double back and get the empty barges. The loaded barges broke a path through the solid ice better than the empty barges. We'd then tie off the empty barges and go with the loaded barges again.

I met the *Missouri* below Lock No. 10 southbound light boat. The captain on the *Missouri* told me he had taken some barges to Genoa and was going back to St. Louis to get another tow. I didn't believe him, but asked him how the ice was above the lock, around McMillian Bend and French Island. He replied, "Oh, not bad—you won't have any trouble with your tow." I knew better, but like a dummy I listened to him.

We got as far as the crossing at French Island and grounded our tow on the ice built up under the tow. In very cold

M/V Rita Barta.

weather, even though you're moving through the water, the broken ice goes under the barges and some freezes to the bottoms. Eventually it may build up to two feet or so thick, so instead of drawing nine feet several of your barges may be drawing eleven feet. We ended up having to break up the tow and take the barges across the reef two at a time. It cost us about twelve hours and a lot of very hard, cold work for the deck crew.

• • •

I used my own judgment the next time. I met the *Missouri* another year in almost the same spot as before. She had the same captain, and he told me the same story about going back to St. Louis. I was sure he was only going back to Dubuque. The *W. S. Rhea* was not too far behind us. At the next lock as I went into the lockhouse to make a telephone call the phone rang and I picked it up. It was our dispatcher, Virgil Granemann, wanting to talk to me. He told me to go on radio silence and not keep our regular radio schedule with the office. We ordinarily called in to the office on a radio schedule twice a day. I was also to ask the lockmen at various locks not to give out our position to anyone.

We went on radio silence and took our tow of six barges on into the Twin Cities and delivered them to the terminal. We then doubled back light boat to find the *Rhea*, who was northbound with twelve loads. We found her just above Lock No. 5-A and split up her tow, taking six loads from her, so we both could get into St. Paul ahead of the *Missouri*, which was right on the *Rhea*'s tail. We had maintained radio silence since we were northbound at Lock No. 9 and didn't use our radio until we were alongside the *Rhea*. The captain on the *Missouri* wanted to know how and why the *Childress* suddenly had a radio. Captain Ivy Sullivan on the *Rhea* told him, "Oh, we brought him some radio tubes." Of course that was a lie.

The dispatcher told me later that the Federal Barge Line dispatcher even called him at home Sunday morning wanting to know where the *Childress* was. He told him truthfully that he had no idea. The last time he'd heard from us was on Friday. The reasoning behind all these shenanigans was strictly economics. At this time the barge lines did not have a lot of extra barges and could not afford to let a bunch of barges lie in the Twin Cities all winter. So the first and second boats into the Twin Cities in the spring got the first loaded tows out ahead of the competition, which made money for the company.

• • •

I have seen ice build up under barges to the extent that one had difficulty getting over a lock sill going into a lock. Usually it happened southbound because of the slower speed.

One winter I was on the *Central* at Lock No. 24 southbound, waiting for the *L. Wade Childress* to lock down ahead of us. When they lowered the *Childress*'s tow down in the lock chamber, it was almost down to the lower water level. All of a sudden we heard wires popping like mad. The tow had so much ice built up under it that some of the barges were sitting on the bottom and the rest were still dropping down. The lock crew had to do a lot of washing before they finally got the ice cleared from underneath the tow and got the tow through the lock. The deck crew had to carry rigging from the boat in order to rewire their tow back together before the boat could depart the chamber.

• • •

I was southbound the last trip of the season and the river was frozen over bank to bank. Just below Wabasha, Minnesota, I caught up with a small tug with two oil barges in tow, practically stopped in the ice. He hailed from Houston, Texas. I called the captain on the radio and asked if it was all right to come around him. He said, "Sure, just come down on the starboard side—there is water all the way over to the head of the island." I told him no, I'd come by on his port side, which I did. He evidently didn't know that there were rock dikes all the way to the island. I think it was his first trip up in that part of the river. He did make it out eventually.

• • •

One November a boat with a three-piece unit petroleum tow was trying to get into Lock No. 5 at an angle. He had the head

M/V L. Wade Childress. *Chief engineer Jim Lear always called her Old Ironsides.*

of his tow in between the lock walls just above the lock gates and was trying to crush the ice up against the lock wall so he could square up and get into the chamber. I don't know where he thought the ice was going to go. He worked at it for a couple of hours and accomplished absolutely nothing while four other southbound tows waited to lock behind him. Finally the lock master called and told him to either break his couplings, so the barges could come into the lock, or back out of the way and let the other boats lock. Some people don't show any common horse sense!

• • •

Some things you learn over the years. Like you don't shove over a reef from deep water without slowing down. One pilot on the *W. S. Rhea* was upbound with fifteen loads at Shokokon Float Light making very good time. The tow sucked down on the reef and hit bottom, causing it to break apart. Nothing was actually aground, the tow simply had sucked all the water out from under it. After doing this a few times you know better. The same thing happened to another pilot on the *Rita Barta* just below the Wapsie River. It happened shortly after midnight when the crew was checking the tow, which they did first thing at every watch change, looking for any loose wires or water in the barges. The tow broke up and four of the barges on the head kept on going. They went upriver and across the head of an island, with one deckhand on the barges. They floated over past the head of the island and the current carried them back out into the channel, down alongside the island to where the *Rita Barta* was backing down and floated them into place in the tow just like we were placing them there. The crew put some wires back on the barges and we proceeded up the river like nothing had happened. The whole show happened in about thirty minutes.

• • •

I saw the same thing happen on the *Rita Barta* at De Soto, Wisconsin, about three one afternoon. We were crossing over to Lost Channel Light with fourteen loaded jumbos and three Lash barges* strung out on the port side back along the boat. When the pilot went over a reef, the last Lash barge broke out of tow. and while we were backing down to retrieve it, the barge started spinning around like a button on a door. The barge spun around the stern of the boat and came up alongside the starboard side of the *Rita Barta* close enough so a deckhand almost jumped over on it. Then the barge changed its mind and went spinning back the other way. Would you believe the barge went back to the port side and fell right back in place where it belonged? The crew laid some wires and we went on up the river like nothing had happened. I would not have believed it if I hadn't seen it.

---

* A Lash barge is a small barge built like a box. It can be loaded at an inland terminal and towed to a deep water port, where it's loaded on a special ship and transported overseas to a port where it's unloaded and towed to its destination without ever having its customs seals broken. This cuts down on stevedoring costs and pilfering.

Sometime in the late 1950s or early 1960s the Valley Line chartered the M/V *Pennsylvania* and I went on her as master. We had a tow from St. Louis to St. Paul, Minnesota. The *Pennsylvania* wasn't all that great a boat. I was coming down the river with fifteen loads at Lock No. 25, and the dam was wide open with the dam gates all out of the water. I was just above the lock about 10:00 p.m. when the chief engineer called up and said we had only one engine; the other had broken a timing chain. I was below any spot where I could back in and catch a line, so I dropped down and caught a line on the lock wall from the head of the tow. I was hoping to make the lock on one engine. The outdraft at the head of the lock was so strong that the crew could not hold the tow and they had to keep slacking off their line. We were lucky that the lock line was long enough so the crew could ease the tow onto the outside lock wall. It landed on the lock wall without breaking any wires. The mate had the tow wired well, and somehow I was able to keep the tow and boat from topping around the end of the outside wall. After some very anxious moments, I was able to work the tow over to the lock wall and make the lock.

The next day I met one of our other boats and told the pilot, Captain Robert Richtman, of my experience. He said "Oh boy! What a boat, I've got to get on her." He asked the office for a transfer and they gave it to him. Bob learned the hard way what a mistake he had made in asking for a transfer to the *Pennsylvania*.

• • •

We were northbound on the Ohio River with the Str. *Tennessee* in open river conditions with a big tow—the barges were rigged six long and five wide. Coming around Evansville bend the pilot was running over the bar on the Kentucky shore, as the river was high. A small motorboat with two people in it came across the river and started to run across ahead of our tow. It got about halfway across the width of the tow when the operator changed his mind and turned to come back to the port side of our tow. He didn't make it and came down on the tow, catching the outside corner of the lead port barge and knocking his outboard motor off into the river. An old white-haired man was in the motorboat with the operator and was either knocked or fell into the river when the motorboat hit the barge. The second man, who was probably in his late twenties, made no effort to rescue the old man. He grabbed the oars and started rowing the boat to the Indiana shore as hard as he could. Evidently he was in shock and scared to death.

This happened about 3:00 p.m. I was awake, lying in bed, and as soon as I heard the danger whistles I ran to the pilothouse. The deck crew on the *Tennessee* was really on the ball and immediately put a yawl over the side. The mate and a deckhand jumped in and started after the old man, who was disappearing beneath the water. I saw the deckhand, who was nicknamed Tennessee, reach down into the water several times, almost a full arm's length, and then he came up with the old man, flopped him into the boat and started to give him resuscitation. Meanwhile I was on the radio phone calling the Evansville emergency squad. (This was before the days of 911.) They responded immediately. I walked out on the bridge wing as soon as I was off the radio and could hear the emergency vehicles coming down the street to the Koch Sand dock, where our yawl was taking the man. They were coming in on the other side of the dock barge as the motorboat was landing. The old man came out of the experience none the worse for wear. Tennessee told me that the water was clear enough that he could see the old man's white hair under the water and was fortunate enough to grab him by the hair. We know the old man worked as a watchman at the Evansville Marina and someone, we know not who, sent both me and the pilot four box seat tickets to the Dade Park Race Track every year for the next twenty-five years.

• • •

In the late 1960s I was transferred to the *Rita Barta*, a 6400-horsepower, twin screw Kort-nozzled. boat, 180 feet long by 54 feet wide with a nine-foot draft, The *Rita Barta* was the boat I broke the thirty-three inches of ice with in Lake Pepin. We ran the Upper Mississippi and Ohio mostly, but at times we made up thirty loaded barges at Cairo and went down on the Lower Mississippi to turn a southern boat, usually in the vicinity of Caruthersville, Missouri. The boats out of the south at this time were the triple-screw, 10,500-horsepower boats such as the M/V *W. J. Barta* and M/V *Lillian Friedman*.

• • •

The joys of piloting! One cold October morning I was south-bound on the Upper Mississippi at French Island with fifteen barge loads of grain. There was a heavy surface fog. I was blowing fog signals and running at reduced speed with the aid of radar. Suddenly, out of the fog, from between the islands came a motorboat with four duck hunters in it. One was running the outboard and the other three were hunched over, trying to stay warm. I blew a danger signal and started backing, trying to stop. The people in the boat never even looked up and they went out of my sight under the head of the tow. The duck hunters made it across in front of me, but

M/V W. J. Barta.
PHOTO BY THE VALLEY LINE

they never gave any indication that they even knew we were around. The main thing on their mind was to be in that duck blind when the sun came over the horizon, so they could start banging away at the ducks come hell or high water.

• • •

In 1977 the company brought out the *L. J. Sullivan*, a twin-screw, 5,600-horsepower Viking Class towboat that had been built at the Dravo Shipyard in Pittsburgh. I went captain on her and spent the majority of my time on the *Sullivan* until I retired at the end of 1980. The *L. J. Sullivan* was a very good boat and would handle twenty-five loaded barges below St. Louis with no sweat—you could even add five empty barges with no problem. The pilot just had to know what he was doing.

We departed St. Louis one Sunday with thirty loaded barges and orders to turn the Lillian Clark in the vicinity of Grand Tower. A new trip-pilot, whom I didn't know, had come aboard that morning at St. Louis. He came on watch at noontime and I went to eat. I came up to the pilothouse after lunch, which I usually did before going to bed. The pilot was crossing over from Michael's Towhead to Lowry Light. He had stopped the engines and was floating. Actually, he was float-

M/V L. J. Sullivan.

ing more sideways than downriver, and if he didn't do something soon, he was going to ground on the head of a sandbar. I told him he'd better come ahead and shove across the
crossing. He backed away from the steering controls and told
me he'd like for me to take her down around Crooks Bend,
which I did. I stayed up with him for the rest of the afternoon. We met the *Lillian Clark* about suppertime and trad-
ed tows. I found out a day or so later when we were northbound that the man had never handled anything more than
a two-barge tow and was scared to death. Luckily, I had him
replaced before he got into serious trouble, but the company had trouble finding a trip-pilot to replace him, so I had to
put up with him until we had gone to St. Paul and back down
to Lock No. 5, where captain Dave Holst relieved him. He
certainly caused me to lose a lot of sleep.

After I retired from the Valley Line Company in December,
1980, I did some trip work for them in 1981, 1982 and the
spring of 1983 on various boats, mostly the *Cincinnati, Lillian
Clark* and *A. D. Haynes.*

18 *The Delta Queen Steamboat Company*

In 1983, Captain Bill Foley, who had been after me for years to come over and help out on the Str. *Delta Queen,* wrote me again. So I went to the Delgado Community College Radar School in New Orleans and obtained the radar endorsement on my pilot license. The Coast Guard required a pilot to have a radar endorsement on his pilot license to pilot a vessel carrying passengers.

In April 1 went to work for the Delta Queen Steamboat Company and began to make some trips on the *Delta Queen.* I felt honored to be on the *Delta Queen.* She was such a grand old boat, with a lot of history behind her. She was fabricated in Glasgow, Scotland in 1924–1925, temporarily assembled, and then the parts were marked and shipped by freighter to a small shipyard at Stockton, California, where the hull was assembled and completed. American workmen installed the machinery and built the upper works and cabins. She was owned by the California Transportation Company, which operated her in the overnight ferry business between Sacramento and San Francisco until 1939. Because of hard times, better highways, and lack of business, the boat was laid up,

176

Str. Delta Queen *blowing a landing whistle at Cincinnati, Ohio.*

along with her sister boat the *Delta King.* When World War II came, the United States used both of them to ferry troops to the ships in the San Francisco harbor. After the war the Maritime Commission took charge of them. The story of how the *Delta Queen* became a Green Line boat operating on the Mississippi and Ohio Rivers and their tributaries is very well documented in *The Saga of the Delta Queen,* by Captain Frederick Way, Jr.

Captains Harold DeMarrero and Charlie Fehlig were masters on the *Delta Queen* when I first started to pilot her. Captain Bill Foley was the other pilot most of the time on the Upper Mississippi, and Captain Harry Louden was my partner most of the time on the Ohio. They were both very good pilots and good partners to work with. I worked on the *Delta Queen* as pilot from Memphis to Pittsburgh and St. Paul.

I met many nice passengers aboard—on almost every cruise there are passengers from foreign countries.

The Delta Queen*'s whistle.*

I worked the *Delta Queen* in 1983, 1984, and 1985, and then in 1986 the company put me on the *Mississippi Queen*. She was the world's largest overnight passenger sternwheel steamboat at that time. She's now outranked by the Str. *American Queen*. Captain Charlie Ritchie was master for several years, and Captain Garland Shoemaker was his relief. When Captain Ritchie left, Captain Lawrence Keeton became master.

My wife and I have many pleasant memories of the days on the *Delta Queen*—like sleeping in a single bed in the pilot's room—and the room was so small that if you turned around fast, you'd meet yourself coming back! The shower and bath was a community affair down the hall, shared by six other people: the two mates, two watchmen and some entertainment staff.

My wife and I would go to bed right after dinner, then we'd get up around 10:00 p.m., dress and go down and dance until minutes before midnight. Then I'd dash up to the pilothouse and go on watch. I usually stood the afterwatch, midnight to 6:00 a.m. and noon to 6:00 p.m.

When I was first on the *Delta Queen* they didn't carry a Riverlorian. Karen "Toots" Maloy came up with the idea, and

Str. Delta Queen.

it was a good one. Before the days of the Riverlorian, the pilots were asked to make comments on various points of interest as we passed them.

One day on the Ohio River we were passing a small church called the Defender Chapel, so named because when it was under construction, the steamboat *Defender* was passing by and its boilers blew up. The *Defender* was a total loss. The bell from the boat was given to the chapel and hangs in the belfry today, hence the name of the chapel. Once I was telling this story on the P. A. system, and no sooner had the words left my mouth when the captain came up to the pilothouse and told me not to do that again. Some of the passengers were very upset and were asking the captain if the *Delta Queen* could blow up! Of course she can't, since she has water tube boilers. I didn't make that mistake again.

During that time we allowed passengers to be in the pilot-house with us while we were underway, which was breaking the law or at least severely bending it. One passenger, Mr. Russ Zahn, used to ride on the bench in the pilothouse for hours

Str. Mississippi Queen. PHOTO COURTESY WILLIAM R. SMITH, GALLIPOLIS, OHIO

on end. If you wished to talk he would hold a conversation with you, otherwise there was never a peep out of him. If you were coming down on a bridge, a close place, or meeting another boat, you'd look around and Russ would have slipped out. He was a joy to have aboard. He really loved the *Delta Queen* and made many cruises each year. One day he came to the pilothouse and said to me, "Captain, I just signed up for five cruises back-to-back for next year and while I was about it I signed up for two cruises for my daughter, son-in-law and grandson. You don't think they will be upset, do you?" I answered, "I'm sure they won't be." He was a great guy.

Every year for the past twenty-five years the Strs. *Delta Queen* and *Belle of Louisville* have had a race during Kentucky Derby Week. Hundreds of people line the banks of the Ohio River to watch the race. The people of Louisville take the race very seriously. One year when the *Delta Queen* won, the people on the wharf really booed us as we came in to hold a ceremony for the awarding of the golden antlers (the winning boat carries the antlers on top of her pilothouse until the next year). The *Mississippi Queen* and the *Delta Queen* also have an annual race from New Orleans to St. Louis. The passengers and crew really get involved in those proceedings.

One year during the race we were tied outside the *Missis-sippi Queen* at Memphis and the maids on the *Mississippi Queen* made a big sign and hung it over the side. It read, "If you can read this sign, you're on the wrong boat." At Natchez-Under-The-Hill, a floozie contest is held on the bank, and everyone troops off the boat, led by the Riverboat Five band. Some of the costumes are outlandish and it's a lot of fun to watch. At other stops the crews and passengers have contests between boat crews. For the last twenty miles below St. Louis, the boats are started out by a starting gun from a Coast Guard buoy boat, and it's a true race to the Eads bridge—always an exciting time for everyone.

On the Delta Queen's *forward deck, cheerleaders cheer the passengers on during the annual race with the* Belle of Louisville.

PHOTO BY AUTHOR

The Riverboat Five leads the parade from the Delta Queen *at Natchez-Under-The-Hill during the Great Steamboat Race from New Orleans to St. Louis.*

PHOTO BY AUTHOR

19 *Mayflies*

On the Upper Mississippi River at certain times of the year we have a hatch of mayflies—or what the river men call "willow flies." They hatch out of the water by the millions. They don't bite or eat anything—just mate and then die. Their eggs fall into the river, go through their life cycle, and hatch again next year. The insects are foul-smelling and make a mess on the boats and around streetlights in river towns. Professor Cal Fremling of Winona State College has been studying mayflies for the past twenty-five or thirty years. He'd leave sample bottles at Lock No. 5-A for the towboats to pick up when they were locking.

We'd take several bottles with us, and whenever there was a big hatch of mayflies, we'd put two or three in a bottle, mark the date and location on the bottle, and then leave it at Lock No. 5-A for Professor Fremling. He has gained a lot of information about the condition and pollution of the river from studying the mayflies, and told me that people have resumed studying them because they're gaining so much information about the various chemicals and pollution showing up in the river.

Professor Fremling was on the *Delta Queen* one trip giving lectures to the passengers about mayflies. One evening, just before sundown, he was in the pilothouse and pointed out to us how the mayflies all fly upstream before they lay their eggs in the water. It was still light enough so we could see swarms of them flying upstream. A very strange phenomenon.

• • •

One evening while we were locking the *Alexander Mackenzie* at Lock No. 24 I went down to the fire room, and the mayflies were very thick. The fireman opened the furnace door, and the draft through the firebox sucked them into the firebox and they burned just like throwing oil on the fire.

• • •

One day I saw the city crew at Clarksville, Missouri, hauling dump truck loads of them to the river. Twice in my life I have seen highway crews at La Crosse, Wisconsin, plowing mayflies off the highway bridge with snowplows. It's hard to believe unless you've seen it. One night in 1949 I told the second mate about seeing the snowplows plowing the mayflies off of the La Crosse highway bridge. He didn't call me a liar, but he certainly thought I could spin a good yarn. A few weeks later we had to tie off our tow at Broken Arrow, an island below La Crosse, to deliver a barge of coal to the Northern States Power plant located up the Black River. The mayflies were very thick. It was about 10:00 p.m. when we came around the bend with one barge, heading up towards the La Crosse highway bridge. I called the second mate to the pilothouse, and when he walked in I handed him the binoculars and told him to take a look. He said, "My ----, there's a snowplow on the bridge, and also a semi truck has jack-knifed." He couldn't get over seeing it; as a matter of fact, he stayed up after he went off watch until we came out of the Black River so he could see if they were still there. He told me he hadn't believed me until he saw it with his own eyes.

• • •

One night on the *Delta Queen* we had a big hatch of mayflies and one lady passenger was really vocal. "Any company who would schedule a trip when there was going to be a hatch of these bugs doesn't know what they're doing." And so on. As if any one can say a year in advance that the mayflies are going to hatch on a certain date, at a certain location.

They hatch at various places. Above Lock No. 19 in Lake Cooper I have seen them on the radar coming out of the water at different locations. They show up like snow on the radar screen. But the morning following a big hatch, the deck crew was always on the ball and had the boat swept and washed down by the time many passengers were up. You had to hunt to find a mayfly on the boat.

• • •

One evening I went into the lockhouse at Lock No. 4 and saw a note telling the lockman to call one of several telephone numbers if there was a big hatch of mayflies. I questioned the lockman and he said that when he called, the Wisconsin Department of Natural Resources people would come down and sweep up a bunch of the mayflies, put them in a bucket of water to release the eggs, and air ship the eggs to Colorado. The DNR people in Colorado were trying to get mayflies started in Colorado streams to improve trout fishing. I never heard how successful they were.

• • •

One night at Lock No. 13 we were locking and the mayflies were really thick, hanging in clusters from the lightposts. All of a sudden something caused them to all fly to the Iowa side of the river and very few were left at the lock except the dead and dying ones. I never did figure what caused them all to leave like that unless the barges bumped the lock wall real hard and made a loud noise.

• • •

I was southbound on the *Rita Barta* with fifteen loaded grain barges, and they were were covered with mayflies. About 8:00 a.m. the sun was shining brightly, but as the tow passed under the Prairie du Chien highway bridge the shadow of the bridge caused the mayflies to take to the air. There was a strong wind blowing on shore, which carried them into Marquette, Iowa. I'm sure the folks there did not appreciate our gift, but being a river town they're used to them, kind of like having high water every spring.

• • •

Years ago I was southbound on the *A. H. Truax* approaching Lock No. 11 at Dubuque, Iowa, and we had a heavy hatch of mayflies. The second mate and a deckhand were standing on the head of the tow ready to make the lock. This deckhand was a talker, always running off at the mouth. All of a sudden I heard him, over the tow speaker, gag and throw up. He said, "Oscar, Oscar—do something, do something." He had swallowed a mayfly. That deckhand learned very quickly to keep his mouth closed when the mayflies were so thick.

20 *Other Stories*

There is a lady named Marie who runs an antique shop located on the riverfront at Burlington, Iowa. She had an old player piano and played it so Teen and I could waltz on the sidewalk in front of her shop. Ranell and I have done the same thing, waltzing in front of her shop. (Teen was my first wife. We were married for almost fifty years when I lost her to ovarian cancer. The following year I met a lovely lady, Ranell, and we have been married for nine years.) Marie has always played the old piano for us every time we stopped at Burlington. In the 1993 flood her shop was badly flooded and the player piano was ruined. The last trip down the year before the flood, Marie had her husband set up his VCR and she played a waltz and fox trot so Ranell and I could dance. Her husband taped us and Marie said they enjoyed the tape all winter. I hope she will able to get the piano repaired—it gave her and the many people who visit her shop a lot of enjoyment.

In the late 1980s the Delta Queen Steamboat Company started to train some female pilots. One was a woman who had worked her way up from the deck on the *Delta Queen:*

Marie PHOTO BY AUTHOR

deckhand, mate, etc. She made a classic statement to me one day: "Oh, this piloting is easy. I've watched these old codgers for years—there's nothing to it." But whenever the wind blew or the weather got bad, she turned the piloting over to the pilot who was training her. I don't think she'd make that statement today. During the high water in the spring of 1988 she stood a watch for part of a cruise on the *Delta Queen*, then quit. I know she can do the job with a little more experience.

• • •

I was pilot on the *Mississippi Queen* in October 1989 and we locked through Lock No. 26, northbound; then southbound we locked through the new Melvin Price Lock, which is 1200 feet long by 110 feet wide and had been opened to traffic while we were up north. It was really rough getting into the lock going southbound. The upper wall was built on a series of cells and there were several feet between the bottom of the lock wall and the water, with a lot of current going under the lock wall. We had to be extremely careful not to get the main deck of the *Mississippi Queen* caught under the wall and also not to hit one of the cells. After the pool is raised, this area will be under water, so it will not bother anyone. In July the *Mississippi Queen* stalled out trying to push up through the old lock chamber—because of high water the current was very swift. We tried using two capstan lines to the lock wall to help pull the boat through the chamber, to no avail. We ended up having the tug *Piasa* help us through the old lock chamber.

• • •

In the spring of 1990, we locked up through the Melvin Price Lock on the *Delta Queen*, and then ran up through the old lock chamber of No. 26. The dam had been blown out, but the lock walls were still there.

• • •

Back in the 1940s on the *Mackenzie*, I was trying to shove up over the pass at Lock & Dam No. 46 on the Ohio River just after the wickets on the dam had been thrown. We were almost over the dam sill when we stalled out. We ran a couple of capstan lines onto the outside of the lock wall and were able to pull ourselves over the sill. Once above the sill, the boat can usually go on without help.

• • •

Captain Nat Haynes on the Str. *Ohio* was stalled out at Sand Creek bar. There was a small cabin on the bank abreast of where he stalled out. He told the mate to go out and talk to an old man sitting in a rocking chair on the porch of the cabin, smoking his pipe and watching the boat. The mate asked the old fellow if it would be all right to put a line on a tree on the bank so they could pull themselves above the tight spot. The old fellow said, "No, you guys have pulled most of my trees out already." I can't blame the old fellow— I'm sure he'd had many of his trees pulled out by various boats, and his riverbank was being cut away with no root system to hold it.

· · ·

We've had many funny incidents occur on the *Queen* boats. One sunny summer afternoon we were proceeding up the Ohio River, running alongside an open field. Suddenly a lady passenger hollered out, "Come quick, come everybody and see the deer, see the deer." She was very excited and was pointing the deer out to the other passengers. I looked out to see a nice herd of about twenty or twenty-five Black Angus cows! Evidently the lady did not know a deer when she saw one.

· · ·

I was on the *Mississippi Queen* coming downstream with a lot of current in the river, which created a strong outdraft at Lock No. 4. The wind was blowing twenty or twenty-five miles per hour on shore. I called the lock on the radio and told them I'd need the lock chamber to be ready for me when I got there, as I'd be unable to hold up in the wind and river current conditions. They said, "Fine, we will have the lock chamber ready for you." When I came around the corner at Beef Slough the lock gates were closed and the lockmen had a red light on against me. I immediately called and they said, "Oh! we had a small fishing boat show up, so decided to lock him ahead of you, before you got here." Well, I went as slow as possible, fighting the wind and current, but the wind quit just when I needed it. The deck crew caught a line on the lock wall, but I knew I'd never be able to straighten up because of the strong outdraft. The stern of the boat was topping out into the river, so I had the deck crew turn the line loose. I told Captain Keeton I'd better flip her and shove back up river and try again. He said, "Do you think you have enough room?" I replied, "I'd better have." I had enough room, but barely, to get topped around above the dam. I shoved back up to Beef Slough, topped around and made the lock the second try. A couple of old ladies down in the lounge were watching the procedure and one said to the other, "Oh, I know what he's going to do, he's going to turn around and back through the lock."

I just wish some of the lockmen would appreciate that we are not kidding when we say we need the lock because of wind and outdraft conditions. You'd think they would understand that, but some of them don't.

• • •

One trip southbound on the *Mississippi Queen*, the office gave us strict orders not to go into Prairie du Chien, Wisconsin, before noon, so the captain told me to kill some time. I said to him, "No problem, I'll just go down to about Clayton, Iowa, turn around and come back up through the lower back channel. That way the passengers can see more of the pretty fall foliage." What is said of the best laid plans of mice and men? We got to Clayton about 10:00 a.m. I started to turn around just as a cold front came through. The wind was blowing straight down the river about ten miles per hour, and then it increased to thirty-five to forty miles per hour as I was half-way turned around. The boat was being blown broadside down the river. As the wind stopped my turning, I called the captain up to the pilothouse to watch my stern for me because the river at this spot is not too wide. The pilot on the *Mississippi Queen,* standing between the controls, cannot see astern at all; he must depend on a watchman standing on the wing bridge to watch his stern. After five attempts at turning around I was fast running out of room, as the channel narrowed considerably just below where we were. We had decided we'd give up and bypass Prairie du Chien, but our last attempt at turning around was successful, and we made it back to our landing at Prairie du Chien about 1:30 p.m. instead of noon.

We always tried to get into Prairie du Chien about daylight, because the wind usually quiets and is practically calm just as the sun is coming up.

(Note: A large florist group was aboard on that trip and they were holding a special show in the Grand Saloon at 10:00 a.m. Unfortunately, the show people didn't have much of an audience once I started my shenanigans—everyone wanted to see what was going on outside!)

21 *M/V President Riverboat Casino*

Captain Philip Ritchie called me in March of 1991 and asked if I would join him in taking the M/V *President* from St. Louis, Missouri, to Davenport, Iowa. The *President* had been in New Orleans at a shipyard being converted from a day excursion boat to a floating gambling casino at a cost of thirteen million dollars. It was an interesting trip. The *President* had originally been a sidewheel steamboat, but when the boilers went bad they had replaced the sidewheels with two Harbormaster units, about 1000 horsepower each. We got to Davenport, Iowa, without incident, except that at Keithsburg, Illinois, the port Harbormaster unit's gear went out. We waited until a small tug from Davenport arrived and assisted us into Davenport. It made a good show, especially for the newspapers. The news media were taking all of their pictures from the Iowa side, showing us limping into town with the tug on the side of the boat.

The state of Iowa had legalized riverboat gambling starting April 1st, 1991, and the *President Riverboat Casino* was the first of the riverboat casinos, so her arrival was big news. Coming up the river we camped out on the *President* as she

M/V President Casino *at Davenport, Iowa, with the city in the back-ground.*   PHOTO COURTESY JUDY PATSCH

had no crew quarters. We also had seventy or eighty con-tractors on board trying to finish up their work so the boat would be ready to operate as a casino on April 1. We did have a very good cook and lots of cots and sleeping bags, so we did all right. When we arrived at Davenport, I went home. (Speaking of Davenport reminds me that Captain L. J. Sulli-van and I brought all the steel for the Centennial bridge up the river in 1941 with the *Alexander Mackenzie*. We landed the barges on the Iowa shore, where the steel was unloaded.)

The day before the *President* was due to start operating as a casino, Captain Don Dobson phoned and asked me to come over and help him out because his pilot had walked off, so my wife and I flew to Davenport. Opening day was full of parades and speeches by politicians and bigwigs. We ran two-hour cruises to nowhere since the river had risen to the point where the *President* would not clear the Centennial bridge or the high line wires at Lock No. 15. We would just leave the dock, go out in the river and hold up. A cruise to nowhere didn't bother the passengers; most of them were down in the Casino playing the one-armed bandits, and the food was good. There were six hundred eighty slot machines aboard plus craps, black jack, roulette and more. I was amazed at the number of passengers who came aboard. There were bus-loads of people from as far away as Chicago, Kansas City and St. Louis. Everyone thinks they're going to win big.

• • •

The *President Riverboat Casino* is operated very differently from other riverboats—at least it was when I was aboard, though I understand it is completely changed now. To start with, they had several departments, a very large restaurant and a buffet. All the food was prepared on the landing or wharf barge, which had a modern galley, then placed aboard for every cruise and served piping hot in the buffet line. The casi-no was a separate operation and had very tight security. There were many supervisors in the casino area—and would you believe that there were thirty-five tons of tokens aboard? We loaded the tokens at St. Louis and they were all placed on one side of the boat, giving us a definite list. The list was correct-ed before we started up the river. All passengers had to pur-chase tokens to play the slots or games. Each ticket had ten twenty-dollar coupons and a buffet coupon attached, which had to be presented in order to eat. The money coupons were used to regulate how much a person could lose on a cruise. At first a person could only spend $200.00 per cruise, but I understand the law has been changed so there's no limit now. The last couple of days I was aboard we had winds gusting to forty miles per hour, but the boat seemed to handle OK—especially with the Harbormaster units, which could be turned in any direction, but quite slowly.

• • •

On one cruise one of the porters or waiters went to one of
the slot machines. (He evidently had been watching the
machine.) He very carefully laid a towel in the coin tray and
then played the machine. After a few tries he hit a big pay-
off. The tokens had hardly stopped falling when two security men appeared, one on either side of him, and he lost his
job. None of the crew on the *President* were allowed to play
the slot machines or gamble on the boat. He should have
known there were security cameras covering every slot,
wheel, and table on the boat. I went through an incredible
security check and all I did was pilot the boat. I was told the
reason was that because of my position, I could go anywhere
on the boat

22 *Str. American Queen*

In 1995, I was scheduled to catch the Str. *American Queen* at Cincinnati, Ohio. She was en route from New Orleans to Pittsburgh to start her inaugural cruise, but she ran into difficulties abreast of Troy, Indiana. She was scheduled to have a photo session at Tell City, Indiana. The company had hired a helicopter to take some pictures of her with Tell City in the background and the sun just coming over the horizon. She was running ahead of schedule, so they nosed her into the bank below Tell City to await daylight. While she was holding up against the bank, the river fell out very fast and caught her aground. The Cannelton locks had shut some dam gates shortly after the *American Queen* had pushed into the bank. Cannelton was not holding any extra water, so they were not able to give the *Queen* a flush to help her off the ground.

My wife, Ranell, and I flew to Cincinnati, where we met with some other crew members and were bused to Troy. We boarded the *American Queen* via a small construction barge and tug that was ferrying people back and forth to the grounded boat. Earlier in the day the barge had been haul-

Str. American Queen *passing Morning Star Landing on the Ohio River, mile 406, en route to Pittsburgh for her inaugural cruise.*

ing garbage and trash from the boat. The mess on the barge hadn't been cleaned up very well, but it did give us transportation to the *American Queen.* That was my wife's first experience boarding a boat by climbing over the railing like climbing a fence in a pasture. We were aground for two or three days. Two small dredges, a backhoe on a barge, and a small towboat with a scraper worked around the *Queen* for a couple of days, making a channel to deeper water. The Coast Guard officers would not allow digging under the boat, just up to her sides. When they had a channel dug and scraped, the *Queen* was slid off the ground and into deeper water by several small tugs pulling on her with the help of a larger towboat that came along at just the right time. We saw it coming and called the captain on the radio and asked if he could help. He called his office and received permission. He tied his tow off and gave us the extra pull we needed. The *American Queen* received a lot of publicity worldwide because of this incident, but no damage.

We went on into Pittsburgh without any more trouble and came out on her inaugural trip on June 27. While we were going northbound, there were three calliope players aboard and they played at every lock, city, town and village we passed through, no matter what time of day or night. I'm sure we awoke a lot of people, because calliope music can be heard for a great distance. At every lock, while we were locking through the entertainment staff put on a little show for the people standing on the lockwalls. Hundreds of people came out to see her at the locks and towns, even in the rain. We saw young people who had climbed trees in order to get a better view, and the bridges were lined with people standing shoulder to shoulder. Where the highway was close to the river, cars were lined up bumper to bumper.

At Pittsburgh the American Queen inaugural ceremony and dedication was a festive affair: music by a band, speeches by dignitaries, and banners and balloons galore. When she left on her maiden voyage, many other vessels shot streams of water into the air and blew their whistles—a grand send-off for a beautiful boat on June 27, 1995—from the same city where the first steamboat on the western rivers, Robert Fulton's *New Orleans*, departed in 1811.

The *American Queen* is big and beautiful and the largest overnight sternwheel passenger steamboat in the world. Southbound, we stopped at many towns where welcoming ceremonies were held and the folks could get a closer look at the boat, although no tours were allowed. The *Queen* is very well appointed inside, with many antiques and paintings. I'm glad I had a chance to work on her before I retired.

· · ·

One of the things I liked best about piloting a boat on the Mississippi River system was that I got to see Mother Nature in all her moods and colors: some of the most beautiful sunrises and sunsets you can imagine; all the trees and flowers budding out in the spring; the hills showing a riot of color in the fall; high water and low; hazy and foggy nights; very windy days; and don't forget the wintertime with ice, snow and very cold weather. It has all made for a very interesting career.

Appendix

My Work Record

During my career on the river I have worked the following boats. This is not in the sequence that I worked them:

M/V *Robert R*	180 hp	single screw
M/V *Resolute*	120 hp	sternwheel
M/V *Sarah McDonald*	180 hp	sternwheel
M/V *Superior Diesel*	75 hp	single screw
M/V *Edw. W. Bilhorn*	240 hp	twin screw
M/V *Bonny R*	240 hp	single screw
M/V *Kenton*	150 hp	single screw
M/V *Kosmos*	240 hp	twin screw
M/V *Keenland - George Stevens*	400 hp	single screw
M/V *Sylvia T*	600 hp	single screw
Str. *Alexander Mackenzie*	1600 hp later 1800 hp	stern wheel
M/V *A. H. Truax*	1430 hp	twin screw
M/V *A. M. Thompson*	2600 hp	twin screw
M/V *Central*	2600 hp	twin screw
M/V *Northern - Peoria*	2800 hp	twin screw
M/V *W. A. Shepard - Wheelock Whitney*	1350 hp	twin screw
Str. *Ohio*	2000 hp	twin screw
Str. *Tennessee*	2000 hp	twin screw
M/V *Indiana*	2000 hp	twin screw
M/V *Louisiana*	2000 hp	twin screw

M/V *Rita Barta*	6400 hp	twin screw
M/V *Lillian Clark*	6400 hp	twin screw
M/V *L. Wade Childress*	3200 hp later 5000 hp	twin screw
M/V *L. J. Sullivan*	5600 hp	twin screw
M/V *Cincinnati*	3300 hp	triple screw
M/V *Dan Luckett*	3200 hp	twin screw
M/V *A. D. Haynes*	6000 hp	twin screw
M/V *Valley Transporter*	6400 hp	twin screw
M/V *Valley Voyager*	6400 hp	twin screw
Str. *Demopolis*	800 hp	twin screw
M/V *L. P. Runkel-* ex-*Monrola*	800 hp	single screw
M/V *Pennsylvania*	3000 hp	twin screw
M/V *Brandon*	2800 hp	twin screw
M/V *Laura H*	120 hp	stern wheel
M/V *LTI-2194*	2000 hp	twin screw
Yacht *Sea Wolf*	1200 hp	twin screw
M/V *Frank C. Rand*	2000 hp	twin screw
M/V *New Orleans*	2000 hp	twin screw
Str. *Delta Queen*	2000 hp	stern wheel
Str. *Mississippi Queen*	2000 hp	sternwheel
M/V *President*	2000 hp	sidewheel propellers
Str. *American Queen*	3000 hp	sternwheel plus two "Z" drives

Glossary

backing and filling means backing and coming ahead with the wheel or wheels—as when trying to wash a hole in the ice.

boat personnel

> **trip-pilot** A pilot who contracts to work a certain number of days or to take a boat from point A to point B.
>
> **roof captain** or **roof-master** The master of the vessel; he does not stand a pilot watch.
>
> **captain** or **master** Usually stands two six-hour watches. He's the highest-ranking person on the boat. If he's a master-pilot, he also stands a pilot watch.
>
> **pilot** Works two six-hour watches opposite the captain.
>
> **wheelsman** or **steersman** Does the steering for the pilot on watch. Usually a person who is learning the river. On an ocean sailing vessel, he would do the steering for the officer on watch and under his orders.
>
> **chief engineer** In charge of the engine room; stands two six-hour watches every twenty-four hours and on call whenever needed.
>
> **assistant engineer** Stands two six-hour watches opposite the chief engineer.
>
> **striker engineer** (oiler)
>
> **deckhands** Two deckhands stand six-hour watches and doubled over when extra hands were needed on deck.
>
> **cook**
>
> **maid**
>
> **galley horse** A man assigned to utility and cleanup work.

capstan A motor-powered vertical drum that winds or releases rope as a winch would.

cathead bitts A set of bitts (posts for securing lines) with a crossbar between them. Usually located on the head deck.

cavel A fitting on a deck to which lines are tied.

dam pool The area above a dam where water is held back.

double lock Locking a tow through a lock a half at a time when the whole tow won't fit in the lock chamber at once. The tow is rejoined when both halves are through.

draft How deep a vessel sits in the water The draft marks are usually painted on the bow and stern of a vessel in six-inch-high numerals, so six inches are left between the numerals.

facing up Wiring a towboat to barges so the boat can steer the barges.

fidley A skylight over the engine room that has a number of windows.

flanking Backing up and letting the current carry the tow where you want it to go.

gage A reference point established by the weather bureau to tell how much water is in the river at a given point.

gate sill The bottom piece that lock gates close against.

head log The cross member at the end of a barge. (The term is from the days of wooden boats and barges.)

headway A boat is making headway when it is moving through the water.

hurdles These use to be made out of piling driven through a woven willow mat laid on the bottom of the river and tied together by other piling and wire rope. They have mostly been replaced by rock wing dams and dikes.

ice gorge Pieces of ice that pile on top of each other and block the flow of current. Piles can be ten or twelve feet high and act as a dam on the river—very dangerous.

"knock out of tow" Unhooking the towboat from the barges.

Kort nozzle A ring around the propeller like a doughnut with about one-quarter inch of clearance from the tips of the propeller blades. A Kort nozzle gives a vessel about

25 per cent more pushing power from the same horsepower engine.

lead line A small rope with fathoms marked by pieces of cloth or leather. Used to measure water depth.

light boat To "go light boat" means for a towboat to travel without any barges attached.

line A line is a rope made out of manila, sisal, cotton or manmade fibers.

   handy line A small line (clothesline weight), about 100 feet long, with a weighted ball (monkey fist) fastened to the end. It is thrown so a heavier mooring line can be attached and pulled over to the boat at a lock or when tying up to a dock.

monkey fist A ball—about the size of a baseball—usually woven from rope and fastened to the end of a handy line or rope to throw to the lockman so he can pull the lock line up and drop it on a mooring pin to aid in locking.

mule training Hooking barges together loosely single file to get through ice more easily. Used when the ice is too heavy to push a tow through.

M/V (motor vessel) A boat usually powered by a diesel engine.

on watch Describes a person who is working. The watches on a riverboat are usually six hours long.

open river Describes a situation in which all the dam gates are out of the water and the dam is not holding back any water. On a wicket-type dam open river means that all the wickets are lying on the bottom of the river and the boats run over the top of them.

outdraft The current flowing across the head of a lock chamber.

point-way Going across the point of a bend rather than following the channel around the deep part of a turn. The point-way is usually shorter and has less current.

possum A big woven bunch of rope to use as a bumper when a boat or barge is coming in to touch the lockwall or dock.

rudders On a sternwheel boat the main rudders are ahead of the paddle wheel and the rudders back of the paddle wheel are called "monkey rudders." On a propeller-powered boat the main rudders are behind the propellers and usually there are two backing or flanking rudders ahead of each of the propellers, one on either side of the propeller shaft.

running the willows Running as close to the shore or bank as possible to escape the current. There is usually less current close to the shore. Pilots call it duck water.

"she" Why a boat is called "she," I don't know, but everyone has their own explanation.

sheer fence A wooden fence made of piling driven into the riverbed and faced with heavy timbers. It directs a vessel into a bridge opening and protects the bridge piers.

sternway Backing or floating downriver backwards.

Str. (steamer) A boat powered by steam generated from a boiler using either coal or oil for fuel.

timberhead A fitting on a deck to which lines are tied.

topping around Turning around to head in the opposite direction.

towing knees Upright structures on the head of a boat used to push on a barge without running under it.

turn a boat To give another boat your barges and take its barges so you both can go back the way you came.

wing dams Usually made of rock or large stones to narrow the river so there will be more current to help scour the channel out, which saves on dredging.

yawl play To "make a yawl play" is to take a small boat (rowboat or motorboat) in to the shore or to another boat.